FINAL CALL...
NOW BOARDING

"This is a much-needed book, which brings great clarity in such a time of false doctrines and deception. I pray that all people of the earth would read it and take it to heart. The Rapture will happen very soon now – believe it or not. I appreciate your work, Jon. Job well done!"

Dr. Mark T. Barclay Founder and Pastor of Living Word Church, Midland, MI and International Speaker

"Final Call presents a refreshing and reader-friendly approach to the often murky subject of the rapture of the Church. You will enjoy Jon Dowler's warm writing style, real-life stories and enthusiastic challenge as he unfolds the Scriptures relating to this all-important topic. Regardless of your current opinion or theological viewpoint on end time events, this book will prove to be an inspiring and thought provoking read. I highly recommend Final Call as we all eagerly await our Lord's return."

Pastor R. Sonny Misar Living Light Church Winona, Minnesota Author of" Journey to Authenticity"

FINAL CALL...
NOW BOARDING

By Jon Dowler

Leeway Literary Works Published by Leeway Artisans, Inc. 9468 Pep Rally Lane, Waldorf, MD 20603

Book & Cover Design by Mykle Lee

ISBN:

Copyright © 04/2010 by Jon Dowler.

No parts of this book may be reproduced or used in any form or by any means, electronic or mechanical, including photocopying, recording, or by any information storage or retrieval system, without permission from the Publisher. All inquires should be addressed to:

9468 Pep Rally Lane, Waldorf, MD 20603. ALL RIGHTS RESERVED

LCCN: Pending

First Edition Printed in the United States of America.

Table of Contents

1 MY FIRST LESSON IN THE RAPTURE 7
Hell Scared out of Me 7
Youthful Lusts and Little Direction 9
Off to College to Seek My Fortune 9

2 MY LIFE-LONG STUDY OF THE RAPTURE WAS ABOUT TO BEGIN 11
A Hunger for God's Word 11
God's Call to Ministry 12
Studying the Rapture at Baton Rouge 13
The Ministry Years 14
A Bitter Pill to Swallow 15
My "Ides of March" 16
Woken With a Mission 17

3 WHAT IS THE RAPTURE? 19
The History of the Rapture 19
The Rapture in Simple Words 21
Debates on When It Happens 22
Faith is Necessary 24

4 THE RAPTURE HAS A PRECEDENT 27
Other Raptures in the Bible 27
Enoch 29
Elijah 31
The Lord Jesus 32
Philip, the Evangelist 32

The Apostle Paul	33
The Apostle John	35
Where's the Church?	36
The 144,000 Jewish Evangelists	37
The Great Multitude	38
The Two Witnesses	39
A Precedent Has Been Set	40

5 KEYS TO UNDERSTANDING END-TIME EVENTS....43

Ask the Important Questions	43
Mankind Divided Into Three Groups	44
The New Testament Letters to the Churches	47
Differences of Judgments	48
The Judging of the Church	48
The Judging of the Nations	49
The Great White Throne Judgment	50
Connection with the Rapture	50

6 ISRAEL AND THE CHURCH 53

God's End-Time Vessels	53
Israel's Plan and Purpose as a Nation	54
Jesus, the Fulfillment of Abraham's Promise	55
A "Church Age" is Clearly Seen	57
Israel's Purpose was clear	59
The Church is Unseen on Earth in the Tribulation	61
The 144,000 and the Two Witnesses	62

7 JESUS' TEACHING ON THE END-TIME EVENTS......65

Answer Questions by Comparing Scriptures	65

Did Jesus Teach the Rapture?	*66*
Jesus' Teaching on the Rapture?	*68*
Lot's Great Escape	*71*
We are Abraham's Seed	*72*
Post/Mid Tribulation Doctrine	
Inconsistent with God's Character	*72*
God Never Changes	*73*
Stunning Similarities of Noah's and Lot's Story	*74*
God's Judgment of Sodom	*75*
Remember Lot's Wife	*76*
Taken or Left?	*77*
Beauties of the Mississippi	*78*
Parable of the Ten Virgins	*80*
The Door Will be Shut	*82*
What Time did it Occur?	*82*
Another Striking Similarity	*83*
We can escape the Tribulation	*84*
Jesus Taught of Rapture and Post Rapture Events	*86*

8 APOSTLE PAUL'S TEACHINGS ON THE RAPTURE ..89

Uniqueness of Paul's Ministry	*89*
The Church at Thessalonica	*91*
The Bible's Most Powerful Pre-Tribulation Rapture Verses	*93*
Initial Signs are the "Braxton Hicks" of End-Time Events	*95*
The Apostle Paul's Mission	*98*
Disbelieving the Rapture Produces Tormenting Fruit	*100*
Untrue Ideals Disturb You Until You Believe Them	*101*

A Falling Away "From Faith" Will Occur   *101*
The "He" Taken Out of the Way   *103*

9 PETER'S TEACHINGS ON THE RAPTURE 105
One of Peter's Most Quoted Verses   *109*
Peter's Final Thoughts on the Rapture   *109*
Peter's Falls Back on Paul's Teachings   *111*
Paul's Teachings Hard to Understand for Some   *112*

10 WHEN WILL THE RAPTURE OCCUR? (PRE, MID, OR POST TRIB?) 113
"So Easy a Caveman could do it"   *113*
I was "Pan-Trib" in Attitude but not Doctrine   *114*
Lack of Persuasion Will "Silence" a Message   *116*
This Message was not for me, but Others   *119*
What event are these speaking of?   *120*
Mid and Post Tribulation Doctrines
Don't Hold Water   *120*
Mid-Tribulation Doctrine   *121*
Post-Tribulation Doctrine   *122*
Not Knowing the Day, Hour, Time, or Season   *122*
Debates can be ended with a Bible and a Calendar   *123*
Buoys on the Water   *124*
The 144,000 and the Two Witnesses   *125*
Mark Off the Days on the Calendar   *126*

11 THE LAST GREAT AWAKENING 129
An Awakening "to God"   *129*
The Awakening That Birthed a Nation   *132*

Nay-Sayers and Judgmentalists   133
God's Judgment Would be Unmistakable   134
Jesus' Message was Awakening   136
Peter Preached About It   138

12 SO NOW WHAT 141
What did Jesus Say?   141
"Watch" and "Pray"   142
We need to be Operating in the Kingdom   143
Don't say, "He's Delaying His Coming"   146
Mid-Trib/Post-Trib Doctrine
Communicates "He's Delaying His Coming"   148

13 GET YOUR BOARDING PASS 153
Final Call…All Boarding   153
Are you on the Passenger Manifest?   154
Jesus is Calling you by Name   154

APPRECIATION

Heartfelt appreciation is given to my best friend and wife, Anita. Without your encouragement and prompting it may have never been! Many thanks to all my friends and church family who encouraged me to cross the finish line. Many thanks also to Jon Larson for his gracious efforts in its final edit. To Mykle Lee and Leeway Artisans Publishing, who caught the vision and partnered with me in seeing it through to publication. Finally, I thank the Holy Spirit for imparting all the revelation and the Lord Jesus for His call, grace and provision to do it."

A Note from the Author

Today, for the most part, prophecy teachers are the only ministers daring to tread on the waters of the Rapture. Many pastors say, "I'm of the Pan-Tribulation theory, I believe it will all pan out in the end." Then they avoid the tough questions, maybe because they don't believe it's their call, maybe because it would cause division, or maybe because they are uncertain themselves.

The message of the "catching away" of the Church has only been taught occasionally to this point. But we have entered a season where this message will go from being taught to being proclaimed and it will be confirmed with signs and wonders.

I am challenging my readers to read this book with a mind open to understanding and truth. I am not teaching the whole book of Revelation or the End-Time events in chronology, but simply show how they all relate, to confirm and demonstrate the purpose of the rapture of the Church. My mission is to show you without contradiction that it is impossible for the pre-tribulation rapture of the Church to not be true. And my goal when you put this book down, is that you will ever be ready for His return, and if you hear anything contrary to this doctrine scriptures will rise up within you describing the event that cannot be explained away.

INTRODUCTION

WHY ANOTHER BOOK ON the Rapture? The word "rapture" is not even in the Bible. There are countless books out on Bible prophecy, and there are even more Bible prophecy teachers on Christian television today. I wrestled with all these questions and thoughts myself. I finally had to settle these things in my heart before I sat down at my computer to embark on this new adventure into unchartered waters.

The first idea for a title of this book was RAPTURE FOR DUMMIES, but I didn't want it to be a derogatory, belittling title. It actually dropped out of my wife's mouth during the conception of the idea for this book. She said, "Jon, there are books for every subject under the sun for dummies, and with what the Lord is giving you, there is no question that

Final Call...Now Boarding

there needs to be one concerning the Rapture that is so simple anyone could understand it."

The title for this book came from an experience I had a number of years ago while waiting to board a flight in the Minneapolis airport. In an airport, television monitors are everywhere displaying times of flight departures and arrivals. As a flight's time of departure approaches, attendants will announce over the intercom that the gates are now open. Soon after, you will begin to hear something like, "All passengers now boarding flight 253 to New York." This will be repeated several times until the inevitable happens, the final boarding call. Once the final boarding call is complete, the staff will enter, the door is closed and locked, and the point of no return has been reached.

On this particular day, I was scheduled for a flight to New York from Minneapolis. I missed all boarding calls because I was talking to my wife on my cell phone. Over my wife's voice, I heard a stern voice over the intercom. "This is the final boarding call for passenger Jon Dowler on flight 253 to New York." The airline staff was making every attempt to ensure that every last person listed for that flight end up on the flight before the doors were closed.

With each call the intensity was increasing, until I was actually called <u>by name</u>. In fact I was the very last passenger.

Jon Dowler

I believe this likeness is at the verge of taking place very soon. I also believe that as the time approaches and the sands of time run out, this message will become more direct and the frequency of it will intensify. The purpose of this book is not only to declare the Rapture, but to equip and enable you to do the same. But before you can fully declare it, you must be persuaded. I believe this book contains the power to do just that.

I have never considered myself a prophecy teacher, only a student of the Rapture in particular. I have probably read one or two books on the subject in my life. I do not even watch End-Time prophecy teachers on television. According to the Church's standard worldwide I would officially be a dummy. That has not been my primary subject matter in 23 years of ministry. So what in the world am I doing writing this book?

In June 2008, I had a supernatural experience through which the Lord told me His return was *very* soon. I can testify to you under oath, <u>Jesus is coming back</u>! For months I never communicated this experience to anyone except my wife and children.

On March 15, 2009 I had a second experience. I was woken at 4:00AM to the voice of the Holy Spirit within me saying, "It is impossible that the Lord Jesus Christ's next return will happen during the Tribulation." Immediately scriptures began to flood my heart showing me why it was impossible. I got

Final Call...Now Boarding

out of bed and was studying the Word on the subject for the next three hours. This book is a result of that experience and the culmination of my life's studies on the Pre-Tribulation and Post-Tribulation return of the Lord Jesus Christ.

Today, for the most part, prophecy teachers are the only ministers daring to tread on these waters as a whole. Many pastors say, "I'm of the Pan-Tribulation theory, I believe it will all pan out in the end." Then they avoid the tough questions. Maybe because they don't believe it's their call, maybe because it would cause division, or maybe because they are uncertain themselves.

The message of the "catching away" of the Church has only been taught occasionally to this point. But we have entered a season where this message will go from being taught to being proclaimed and it will be confirmed with signs and wonders.

I challenge you to continue reading this book. I am not teaching the whole book of Revelation, or the End-Time events as a whole. Instead I am teaching how each relate to confirm and demonstrate the purpose of the rapture of the Church. My mission is to show you without contradiction, that it is impossible for the Pre-Tribulation Rapture to **not be** true. I know there are many contrary things being taught. My goal when you put this book down, is that you will ever be ready for His return, and if you hear anything contrary to this doctrine, scriptures will rise up within you describing the event that cannot be explained away.

CHAPTER 1

MY FIRST LESSON IN THE RAPTURE

I WANT TO START THIS FIRST LESSON with the very basics, not assuming that every reader is even familiar with the Rapture experience. Easily stated, this earth is on a timeline and there are certain events that will happen, without a doubt. When the sands of time run out we are going to move on with our spiritual destiny.

Hell Scared out of Me

I was first exposed to the idea of the Rapture in the early seventies when End-Time events were a hot issue. The book the <u>Late Great Planet Earth</u> was a best seller and <u>Holy Joe</u> comic style tracts were very

Final Call...Now Boarding

popular. Literature like these depicted the Rapture, and the great tribulation, however I'll admit that I never read much of them.

I was about seven years old at the time when my family attended a Church of God in Melbourne, Florida. I don't know if it was a wide-spread move in the whole body of Christ, but at our church we had frequent movie nights – popcorn was not included! I recall a series of movies which depicted the Rapture taking place, and the consequences for those who were left behind on earth. To be frank, these movies literally scared Hell out of me. The Rapture was portrayed as the "great escape" from all the calamity that was coming on the earth. Millions of people suddenly vanished, and any of those remaining that not deny the Lord Jesus were beheaded. I also remember other movies of the movies did not depict the Rapture at all and the Church was shown going through the Tribulation.

After studying End-Time events, I found that there were a number of things in these movies that were not scripturally accurate. Scripture teaches that the Church is to be a victorious overcoming entity, and she will depart from earth with a blaze of glory. These movies

portrayed the Church being a defeated fearful entity upon the earth. But *my* they were convincing. Even with their limited knowledge, they managed to get the message out of living "ready" to meet the Lord. And as a result I received Jesus as my personal Lord and Savior. Whatever the means, right or wrong, correct or incorrect, it worked with me.

Youthful Lusts and Little Direction

From grade school through high school years I could not deny the realness of the Lord to me but the fear of God's wrath had waned. At age 16, I was living like a typical youth, involved in things that would make me blush now. At age 17 I met my future wife Anita, the love of my life, and the first part of my destiny being fulfilled. There was a part of me that had a hunger for the things of the Spirit. I knew there was more.

Off to College to Seek My Fortune

When I set out for college first I was going to be a lawyer, then a mechanical engineer –Iowa State denied my acceptance, so I attended Northern Iowa as a math major with a minor in teaching, or so I thought. I was on my way to college, as my grandma would say, "to seek my fortune." Then my life was changed.

In my bedroom at 2:00 in the morning, in the middle of spring break, in 1985, I was introduced to the third person of the Godhead, the Holy Spirit. He then became, and still is, my friend, my favorite teacher and professor of all time, and that's what Jesus said He would be (John 14:26). Little did I know all He was about to show me, and that my life would never be the same.

Chapter 2

My Life-Long Study Of The Rapture Was About To Begin

A Hunger for God's Word

AFTER SPRING BREAK and my encounter with the Holy Spirit, my outlook on life and what I valued seemed to change. Anita, my future wife, was attending school with me and she will attest to this fact. I had an insatiable desire and hunger to read the Bible, especially the New Testament epistles.

One way I could describe the hunger was like a youth getting a new cutting age video game. No matter what they are doing or where they are, they are consumed with playing it. If they can't play it, they are thinking about playing it. They can't wait to get home from school to play it. They will even miss watching TV to play it. They talk about the game to their friends. They'll miss a meal to play it. They'll wake up early to play it. They'll stay up late into the night to play it, with no thought of the consequences of the lack of sleep. That's what happened to me.

The New Testament books, Matthew through Revelation, were where I spent every free moment. On campus I had a book bag in which I carried all of my class books, however my Bible I carried in my hand. When you'd have expected to find me studying for classes I would have my Bible in my hand. Up until this point in my life I had only heard Jesus was coming back, but now I was beginning to stumble upon scriptures in my studies which pointed to this event.

God's Call to Ministry

In July, I went to Maine to visit my mother's family in Machias. I was reading my Bible late one evening from the eighth chapter of the book of Acts, and I had an amazing experience in which the Lord spoke to my heart saying, "Feed my sheep." There was more to this experience but that will have to be another book. I still have that Bible and the pages of Acts chapter 8 are still wavy from all the tears that were shed that night and the call of God finally became real to me.

The following Sunday, I saw an advertisement for the Jimmy Swaggart Bible College. As I watched it, I heard the words, "When the next semester starts in 4 weeks, you will be in Baton Rouge." That was beyond comprehension for me because I was already enrolled at the University of Northern Iowa for the fall semester, not to mention, what my parents would think when they learned of this "revelation." It was not easy but I was obedient, and when the new semester began I was in Baton Rouge, just as He had told me! Wow!

Studying the Rapture at Baton Rouge

After getting settled in Bible college, I had a handful of close friends, and we had a strange custom while at meal time in the cafeteria. We would simulate Jimmy Swaggart's daily broadcast, "Study in the Word." My friend and I would start, introducing us as guests on the panel for that day's broadcast discussion. We would proceed to discuss hot theological topics and it was at one of these sessions that certain questions arose.

"Is there a Rapture? When will it take place? If it does take place, when will it happen? Before the Seven-Year Tribulation? During the Seven-Year

Tribulation? At the end of the Seven-Year Tribulation?"

Some of my friends were bringing up opposing views to what I believed was the truth. I wondered if I should respond by saying, "It will all pan out in the end." I had always lived with an expectation the Jesus could appear at any moment. That moment I was resolved to search out and answer these question for myself. Over the next few nights and weeks I did answer these questions from scripture to my own satisfaction.

The Ministry Years

From Baton Rouge I went on to start and pastor two different churches from 1986 to 1997. During that time, I did study End-Time events in phases, but rarely taught on them. I never fully taught on the book of Revelation and had no prolonged efforts of preaching on the rapture of the Church or Christ's return. I would resist it. I would say, "Leave that for the Bible prophecy teachers."

I went on in 1998 until the present to serve under other men of God, and continue to seek out and follow God's plan. I did not know it, but in March of 2009, God was about to bring something to pass, something new in my ministry, and it was all about to come to a head.

Jon Dowler

A Bitter Pill to Swallow

Our home church has Life-Groups that meet between Sunday morning services. Our leader asked me to teach one. Our church's Life-Group had been going through the book of Luke in verse by verse study. I responded with a enthusiastic "yes." But when I began to prepare for my teaching, I saw that my session would cover Luke 21, verses 5-38. I thought, "End-Time events, great, this is just what I needed....why can't someone else teach it." I wrestled with it for days, wishing it would go away.

Our church is an awesome body of people. We literally are a melting pot of Christianity. When it comes to End-Time events there are a number of different beliefs among our members. Our church members walk in a degree of love that we will not make a major doctrinal issue about minor doctrinal differences. Much of the Church world could stand to learn a lesson in this. As one of my fathers in the faith said it this way, "We need to major in the majors and minor in the minors."

My frustration with teaching the lesson continued. I have some very strong beliefs concerning the Rapture and End-Time events, and I didn't want to rock anyone's boat. I did not want to come across as a know it all, nor did I want to compromise what I believe the Bible to say. My wife ended up silencing me saying, "You need to just teach what the Bible says nothing more, nothing less. You are always saying you want God to use you, well shut-up and get with it." She didn't actually say "shut-up" but I heard it in her voice.

To make a long story short, the time for the lesson came and most of the teaching was focusing on what Jesus was speaking to Israel as it pertained to Israel. I touched on the Rapture at the end of the lesson and it was surprisingly painless! I learned that the subject of teaching on End-Time events could be interesting and that there was a genuine hunger in the people to hear what the Bible teaches concerning the subject.

God's word has the answer and can speak relevantly to all the current issues of the day. It will also bring great peace and joy when it is received with an open heart.

My "Ides of March"

Julius Caesar was assassinated on March 15, 44 B.C. which became known as the "Ides of March." That date and studying the events of that date has intrigued people for centuries. It was literally a day that changed a society and the world.

Interestingly enough, my next experience occurred on this very date, March 15, 2009. Does that date have prophetic significance? I would say no, but what it represents in my life does. Am I going to mark this as a date in which something prophetic is going to happen? Absolutely not! Many things have been propagated in God's name concerning the Lord's return. Understand that anytime anyone ascribes dates in connection to His return it is unscriptural. Scripture does not reveal that or teach a specific date. I do, however, believe there is some significance applicable here as to the Ides of March.

I know that the revelation I received early that morning marked a day of abrupt change in me. The understanding I received that day was concerning a future event. I believe that when that event occurs, it will set off a ripple of repercussions throughout society and beyond, and we need to be ready. This message which is rarely mentioned or taught is about to be declared, preached, and proclaimed like never before.

Woken With a Mission

The morning of March 15, I would have preferred to sleep substantially later. Prior to that morning I attended a men's conference in which I was one of the speakers. I had gotten only about two hours of sleep over two days. But at 4:00AM that morning I was woken suddenly and heard these words in my

Final Call...Now Boarding

spirit, "It is...IMPOSSIBLE... for Jesus next return to earth to happen during the Tribulation."

Immediately, page after page of scripture appeared before my eyes in what seemed to be a matter of seconds. These were all scriptures that I thought I knew, but I was seeing them in a completely different light. I thought, "I need to grab my Bible and look at these verses." I already believed that the Rapture was biblically accurate prophetically, but with this increased revelation, a responsibility dropped on my shoulders, and a commission. This experience was not happening for me to know, but as a mandate to tell others!

At once I got out of bed grabbed my Bible and notebook, and for the next three hours, I turned from scripture to scripture. As I did, light after light turned on inside of me. The next several weeks, I was obsessed in spending every spare moment of time studying and rooting myself in these revelations. Bashfulness, timidity, and a lack of urgency were replaced with boldness, certainty, and a fire.

To this point I have not taught on any scripture. I have only provided a back drop of my life and experience. I am just a normal person, but my beliefs on this subject are a culmination of my life to this point. These beliefs have transformed me to the point where they are no longer my beliefs, but they are my life.

Chapter 3

What Is The Rapture?

The History of the Rapture

THIS FUNNY SOUNDING WORD "rapture," where did it come from? Many unchurched people or people with no connection to the Christian faith have at least heard of that term. One of the arguments of people who do not believe in this experience will say, "That word is not in the Bible." I fully agree with that statement. We will talk about that later, but first things first.

The <u>American Heritage Dictionary</u> gives these definitions of the word "rapture:"

1. The state of being transported by a lofty emotion; ecstasy.
2. An expression of an ecstatic feeling.

3. The transporting of a person from one place to another. (Italics added)

With that said, I would like to set a precedent from this point forward. Gleaning truth from the third definition provided to us here, anytime I use the word rapture throughout this book, I am referring to a *supernatural* "transporting of a person from one place to another," nothing more, nothing less.

Some of the seeds for the "idea" of the Rapture were introduced in 1690 through Francisco Ribera, a Jesuit priest, who published a commentary on the book of Revelation in the Bible. He believed that the End-Time prophecies and judgments written in the book of Daniel and Revelation in the Bible were not for the Church's age or dispensation, but for the final seven years of time, referred to as the Great Tribulation.

The word "rapture" was coined and became popular in the late 19th century in America through an Irish evangelist, John Nelson Darby. In 1878 William Blackstone's book, Jesus is Coming, sold more than a million copies over the next several decades, and also taught of a secret rapture of the Church.

Jon Dowler

The Rapture in Simple Words

The Rapture is a name that has been coined to describe a biblical event in which the Lord Jesus Christ will come back to earth, not to stay, but gather His body, the Church. Let me now explain what the Church's rapture will look like when it happens.

The Lord Jesus will return to gather His saints. In an instant, the bodies of saints who preceded us in death will be resurrected, and will simultaneously have their physical bodies transformed with the saints still living. They will be immediately caught up to meet the Lord, and be transported to heaven. This will happen at the speed of lightning, and without warning.

This event, without debate, is described in scripture. Some may choose not to believe, it but nevertheless it is in scripture. Read what the Apostle Paul wrote in one of his letters to the Church at Thessalonica:

> "...We believe that Jesus died and rose again and so we believe that God will bring with Jesus those who have fallen asleep in Him. According to the Lord's own word, we tell you that we who are still alive, who are left till the coming of the Lord, will certainly not precede those who have
>
> fallen asleep. For the Lord himself will come down from heaven, with a loud command, with the voice of the archangel and with the trumpet

> call of God, and the dead in Christ will rise first. After that, we who are still alive and are left will be caught up together with them in the clouds to meet the Lord in the air. And so we will be with the Lord forever. Therefore encourage each other with these words." (1 Thessalonians 4:1418 NIV)

And again in a letter to the Church at Corinth:

> "Listen, I tell you a mystery: We will not all sleep, but we will all be changed— in a flash, in the twinkling of an eye, at the last trumpet. For the trumpet will sound, the dead will be raised imperishable, and we will be changed. For the perishable must clothe itself with the imperishable, and the mortal with immortality. When the perishable has been clothed with the imperishable, and the mortal with immortality, then the saying that is written will come true: "Death has been swallowed up in victory."(1 Corinthians 15:51-54 NIV)

I will fully expound these verses in Chapter 8.

Debates on When It Happens

Most Christians believe in this experience, however debate arises on the chronological timing of the event. This is the reason for this book. Why? To win an argument? To attempt to justify my doctrinal belief and prove others wrong? To have a bunch of converts who can just spew this doctrine? So all the believers can stand around looking into the clouds just looking for Him? So believers can pile up credit card debt thinking they'd never have to pay it? By the way, that really has happened! Because I just believe in an "escapist" doctrine, and I don't want to have to endure the Tribulation? No, no, no, a thousand times, NO!

The reason is the Bible teaches this event and shows the chronological order of End-Time events, the Rapture, the Tribulation, and Jesus' return to establish His kingdom on the earth. Does it explain them in one chapter? That would be neat, tidy, and convenient, but even then people would not believe. We have to compare scripture with scripture. As we do, it is apparent that certain events described in scripture cannot be the same thing, it is impossible! As we go through events, these issues will be addressed and explained.

Again you may be asking, "Why this book then?" The Rapture is part of God's purposes and plans for the ages. Our destiny is tied up in this message, and so is Israel's. The heart of this message is tied to living for Him every moment of our lives. It is a message that purifies. We are at the verge of this message being lost from the Church. The Lord has caused a stirring at certain times throughout the past decades to bring this message to the forefront. He has even appeared to men and told them, "Tell my people I'm coming back!" The message would go and years later it would wane. He could come in my lifetime, in my children's lifetime, or maybe in my great-grandchildren's. I believe it is going to be sooner rather than later, however, this message cannot wane, it cannot be lost from future generations or fall by the wayside. In obedience to the call, I am writing on.

Please allow me to put out my disclaimer here. Let it be known…I am a preacher, but I do not want this book to come across in a way in which you feel you were being preached at. My life has been a journey in which I have studied this event in different phases. I simply want to share the results of my studies as simply as possible, in a manner which is almost irrefutable. "Almost" you ask?

Faith is Necessary

In my continuing journey to seek after and understand God and His ways, I have found that one law has always been consistent. It's the law of faith. Any of God's communications with man through the Bible or otherwise require some element of faith for the picture to become complete.

The Bible actually says, "Without faith is it impossible to please Him."(Hebrews 11:6) God may paint 70% or 98% of His plan in the Bible, but whatever the missing part is we must step out by faith and believe the things He has said and not be as concerned about what He has not said.

I have learned that the more we hear and understand what the Bible teaches, the missing percentage grows smaller and smaller. The apostle Paul said it this way, "Now we know in part." When we come to know the part, we can believe the rest into being.

God has provided the chronological "skeletal structure" for the End-Time events. Every person may never know what every symbol in the book of Revelation means. We may never know every detail, but the structure is clearly outlined, and that is what we are about to look into.

Chapter 4

The Rapture Has A Precedent

Other Raptures in the Bible

AS I JUST TYPED THAT sub-heading, I can hear people shouting "Heresy... heresy... false doctrine!"

If you remember in the last chapter, I told you that my definition of rapture was a *supernatural* "transporting of a person from one place to another." We could even say "translation" as another term. Has anyone ever been supernaturally transported from one place to another in the Bible? Has this happened more than once? Does the "Rapture" have a precedent in the Bible? In this chapter, you will see instances of people being supernaturally transported from one place to another on earth, and even from earth to heaven.

If you were to do an exhaustive study on any given subject of the Bible, you will find that God has always related to man in a consistent manner, and that many precedents have ALREADY been established. Through our lack of understanding, or being improperly taught, we can simply accept an assumption that just isn't so. Our coming to understanding those precedents will persuade us, and actually impart faith to us. One of those common catch phrases those doubting the Rapture parrot is, "The word rapture is not in the Bible, it's unscriptural."

Utilizing my definition of the word rapture as the supernatural "transporting of a person from one place to another," the Bible definitely has a precedent! "How many times" you may be thinking. One time? No. Two? No. Five? No. Eight? I will show you a total of TEN times including the rapture of the Church! You may be thinking, "But I never knew those were there." That's is why this book was written.

If someone thinks, "Well that was back in Bible days and it won't be happening now." Four of those raptures haven't occurred yet but are clearly prophesied and are still yet to be fulfilled. If God raptured people in the past, and His word indicates that He's going to rapture people in the future, then it is definitely not far fetched to believe that the Church will experience the Rapture!

In our judicial system, when a ruling is made concerning a case where the intent of the law comes into question, prior cases are examined to see if any precedent has been set to even justify or endorse a particular ruling or judgment. Here are some of the other cases I would like to submit to you as evidence that the Rapture is not as far-fetched as you might think.

Enoch

Enoch is the first of my examples. Not much was said about him in the Bible. Even so, here is our first example of someone being here one moment and being gone the next. In Genesis 5:24 the scripture tells us:

> "And Enoch walked with God, and <u>then he was not</u>, for God took him."(Modern King James Translation, underline added)

The New Testament also refers to this event in Hebrews 11:5-6:

> "By faith Enoch <u>was translated so as not to see death</u>, and he was not found, because God had translated him; for before his translation he had this testimony, that he pleased God.

> But without faith it is impossible to please Him, for he who comes to God must believe that He is and that He is a rewarder of those who diligently seek Him."(Modern King James Translation, underline added)

These scriptures state that "by faith Enoch was translated so as not to see death." Sounds like the Rapture doesn't it? Why did it happen? Because his testimony was that he pleased God. He lived 365 years and the last 300 of those years he walked with God. (Genesis 5:22)

Just a side note, how did he please God? He was living by faith. Our original text in Hebrews 11:6 states, "Without faith it is impossible to please Him." It was a life of faith and believing that enabled him to be translated and never see death.

As with any examples we use from the Old Testament, they do have New Testament significance. Referring to the Old Testament patriarchs the Apostle Paul wrote, "And all these things happened to them as examples." (1 Corinthians 10:11, New King James Version) In the book of Hebrews, it is stated that the Old Testament shadows and types serve as "...copies

and shadows of the heavenly things..." (Hebrews 8:5, New King James Version).

Case and point, Enoch was the first person to be raptured or translated in the Bible. What also is interesting is that the Apostle Jude even quoted one of the things Enoch had prophesied in Jude verse 14, "Behold the Lord comes with ten thousands of His saints." This not referring to the Rapture, but in reference to His return at the end of the Seven-Year Tribulation, with His saints with Him I might add. Enoch was the first person recorded in the Bible to preach "Jesus is coming back."

Elijah

Elijah is our next example of one being "caught up" in the Old Testament. The thing that he had in common with Enoch is that throughout his life he "walked with God," and we can actually see substantial dialogue he had with the Lord. We know that his "translation" must have even been prophesied beforehand. In 2 Kings 2:5 the sons of the prophets made this statement to his servant Elisha saying, "Do you know that Jehovah will take your master away from your head today? And he answered, 'Yes, I know. Keep silent.'"(MKJV) It is also amazing to see how this event was described in this chapter prior to occurring. "And it happened when Jehovah was to take Elijah up into Heaven by a whirlwind…" (2 Kings 2:1 MKJV)

Elisha his servant was relentless and insistent about being present when it happened and he did witness it with his own eyes. In 2 Kings 2:11, the

Final Call…Now Boarding

Bible describes that, "it happened as they went on and talked, behold, a chariot of fire and horses of fire came, and they separated between them both. And Elijah <u>went up</u> in a tempest into Heaven." (MKJV Underline added)

Let's move on to New Testament examples of being "caught up."

The Lord Jesus

After Jesus was resurrected, He spent a forty day period with them on the earth before ascending to heaven. We can see this account in Acts 1:9, "…As they watched, He was taken up. And a cloud received Him out of their sight."(MKJV) After this two angels appeared to them and said, "This same Jesus <u>who is taken up from you into Heaven</u>, will come in the way you have seen Him going into Heaven." (Chapter 1 verse 11, MKJV Underline added) Case in point three, Jesus was caught up to heaven.

Philip, the Evangelist

Philip, the evangelist, was the next example of someone being caught up and being supernaturally transported in Acts 8:26-40. Many refer to Philip as being "translated," and I have no argument with that term. In discussing the Rapture, however, remember the dictionary definition I have adopted is being "supernaturally transported" from one place to another.

Philip had preached in Samaria, and afterward an angel appeared to him and told him to go south toward Gaza. The Holy Spirit told him to run to a chariot that was parked and an Ethiopian was sitting there reading the scriptures. Philip preached the gospel to him and he believed and received it. Upon coming on some water, Philip baptized him in the water. Then the Bible states:

> "And when they had come up out of the water, the Spirit of the Lord caught Philip away, so that the eunuch saw him no more..." (Acts 8:39 underline added MKJV)

Philip did not go to heaven, but the next place he was seen was in Azotus which was about 30 miles away.

The Apostle Paul

In his second letter to the Church at Corinth, the Apostle Paul describes his rapture experience.

> "I know a man in Christ fourteen years before (whether in the body, I do not know; or outside of

the body, I do not know; God knows) such a one was caught up to the third Heaven." (2 Corinthians 12:2 MKJV, underline added) "That he was caught up into Paradise and heard unspeakable words, which it is not allowed for a man to utter." (2 Corinthians 12:4 MKJV, underline added)

Paul was literally caught up to Heaven or paradise.

Let's pause here for a second. For any who do not know this, all of our New Testament epistles that we read today were originally written in the Greek language. Many of our English versions are direct translations and some are paraphrases. The most quoted scriptures concerning the Rapture are 1 Thessalonians 4:16-17, "For the Lord Himself shall descend from Heaven with a shout, with the voice of the archangel and with the trumpet of God. And the dead in Christ shall rise first. Then we who are alive and remain shall be caught up together with them in the clouds, to meet the Lord in the air. And so we shall ever be with the Lord."(MKJV, underline added)

The word in the Greek is the exact same word that Paul used in 2 Corinthians 12:2-4 to describe himself being caught up into heaven. It is also the same word used to describe Philip being caught up. There is a common thread here. Paul did not choose his words randomly. He only used that Greek word "harpazo" three times in his writings, and each instance was in these three scriptures we just quoted. Thayer's Greek Definition defines this word as: To seize, carry off by force, to seize on, claim for one's self eagerly, to snatch out or away.

Paul had to have revelation concerning this word and specifically intended how he used it. To me, this speaks volumes to validate the Rapture experience.

The Apostle John

The Apostle John is probably my favorite. It occurs in the book of Revelation chapter 4, verses 1 and 2.

> "After these things I looked, and behold, a door was opened in Heaven. And the first voice which I heard was as it were of a trumpet talking with me, saying, Come up here, and I will show you what must occur after these things. And immediately I became in spirit. And behold, a throne was set in Heaven, and One sat upon the throne."(MKJV)

This particular experience occurred immediately following instruction from the Lord to the seven churches. There are striking similarities between this experience and Paul's "catching up" experience, and even when Paul described the Church's rapture. Let's describe John's experience (Revelation 4:1,2) with the Apostle Paul's account (1 Thessalonians 4:16,17) we just looked at.

Final Call...Now Boarding

- Paul - "The Lord Himself shall descend from Heaven with a shout, <u>with the voice of the archangel</u> and <u>with the trumpet of God...</u>"
- John - "And the first voice which I heard was as it were of a trumpet talking with me, which said, Come up hither"
- Paul - "Then we who are alive and remain shall be <u>caught up</u> together with them."
- John - "And <u>immediately I became in spirit</u>." And behold, a throne was set in Heaven, and One sat upon the throne."

Do you see the comparison of these two from the references in 1 Thessalonians chapter 4 and Revelations chapter 4?"

Where's the Church?

Before we move on I would like to plant a seed here. After these words in Revelation chapter 4, the word "church" does not occur again until Revelation 22:16. What happened to the Church? We will refer to this again in further in the book, however this has major significance and implications.

Now let's look at future raptures that the Bible records and prophesies. Have you ever heard of such a thing? Yes, it is in the Bible. This is why the apostle John said, "...Blessed (happy, to be envied) are those that hear [it read] and who keep themselves true to the things which are written in it…" (Revelation 1:3 Amplified version)

The 144,000 Jewish Evangelists

The book of Revelation teaches that there will be 144,000 evangelists. This also is very significant to the purposes of God being fulfilled on the earth. We will refer to them later in the book because they again enforce the Pre-Tribulation rapture of the Church. For the sake of this discussion, however, the purpose is to show you that they will be "caught up." They will be raised up as an army of preachers and commissioned by the Lord for approximately the first 4 years of the Tribulation. When their mission is complete, they will suddenly appear in heaven.

> "And I looked, and lo, <u>the Lamb stood on Mount Zion</u>. And <u>with Him were a hundred and forty-four thousands</u>, having His Father's name written in their foreheads…
>
> "And they sang as it were a new song before the throne and before the four living creatures and the elders. And no one could learn that song except the hundred and forty-four thousands who were redeemed from the earth." (Revelation 14:1,3 MKJV, underlines added)

Final Call...Now Boarding

That leads us to our next "catching up," the harvest of the 144,000 Jewish Evangelists. Let us keep moving!

The Great Multitude

The book of Revelation refers to a great multitude, <u>not the Church</u>, but a great multitude that appears in heaven. Let's read the verses:

> "After these things I looked, and lo, a <u>great multitude</u>, which no man could number, <u>out of all nations</u> and kindreds and people and tongues, stood before the throne and before the Lamb, clothed with white robes, with palms in their hands....
>
> "And <u>one of the elders answered</u>, saying to me, <u>Who are these </u>who are arrayed in white robes, and from where do they come?
>
> "And I said to him, Sir, you know. And he said to me, <u>These are the ones who came out of the great tribulation</u> and have washed their robes, and have whitened them in the blood of the Lamb. (Revelation 7:9,13,14; MKJV underline added)

Did it happen, or should I say, will it? Oh yes, it will! Was that the last occurrence? No, we have one final instance to look at. So let's continue.

The Two Witnesses

God will send two witnesses during the last three and a half years (forty-two months) of the Tribulation. These 'witnesses" will be prophets and they will be testifying God's word. They will be virtually unstoppable until the very end. They will have power to turn waters to blood, to cause no rain to fall and to cause plagues to come on earth at will. They will consume their enemies with fire from their mouths. (Revelation 11:1-6) Sounds like something from the X-Men doesn't it?

When their preaching is finished, the beast will make war with them, overcome them and kill them, only because their mission is complete. They will lie dead in the street for three-and a-half-days. Then God breathes life into them and they'll be resurrected. Then look at what happens:

> "And after three days and a half, a spirit of life from God entered into them, and they stood on their feet. And great fear fell on those seeing them.
>
> "And they heard a great voice from Heaven saying to them, Come up here. And they went up to Heaven in a cloud, and their enemies watched them. (Revelation 11:11,12 MKJV underlines added)

Final Call...Now Boarding

I want to again point out to you that this was the same verbiage used in Revelation 4:1-2. "They heard a voice" saying "Come up here." This cannot be coincidence. We can clearly see a pattern.

A Precedent Has Been Set

There is a precedent. The supernatural transporting of a person is not as hard to find as some would have you think. Even though this book is dedicated to proclaiming the rapture of the Church, this whole chapter was dedicated to raptures and not even one of them was the rapture of the Church. Of all of these examples, I have tallied a total 144,008 plus people being transported supernaturally not including the size of the Great Multitude.

Our eyes must be opened to these truths. These revelations and their evidence is overwhelming. As I wrote this chapter, I had the sense that I was presenting a case before the jury. Were Enoch, Elijah, and Jesus taken up into heaven? Yes, then it is in the Bible! In the future, are the 144,000 Jewish evangelists and the two Witnesses going to suddenly be taken up to heaven supernaturally? Are both of these events that will come to pass? Absolutely yes. If it happened in the past, and Scripture clearly prophecies that it happens again in the future, then it is definitely not a far-fetched notion for us to believe for ourselves today.

The scriptures we examined concerning Enoch said that, "By faith Enoch was translated that he should not see death."(Hebrews 11:5) I want to follow his example of believing God, and the Bible should be the basis and foundation of our belief system. Jesus said, "…When the Son of Man comes, will he find faith on the earth."(Luke 18:8 God's Word Translation) Let's be honest and make sure we are in faith when he returns. I strongly encourage you to study these instances again on your own. God is not withholding information. He wants us to understand, especially if you are a believer in the Lord Jesus Christ. Jesus said it this way, "To you it is given to know the mystery of the kingdom of God." (Mark 4:11 Modern King James Version) Let's go on and receive more understanding from God's Word.

Chapter 5

Keys To Understanding End-Time Events

Ask the Important Questions

THE STUDY OF THE END-TIME events has brought much confusion to the Church worldwide. I have even watched television shows and podcasts where ministers attempt to teach on Bible prophecy. Unintentionally, everything gets lumped into the same pile, confusion sets in, and multiple events which scripture teaches get described as a single event. This is not rightly dividing the scripture.

Once again I would like to make a disclaimer. Many ministers teach things contrary to what I am teaching. I am not attempting to convert any of them to "my" doctrine. They are free to believe and teach what they would like. My desire is to show what the Bible says concerning the Rapture in such a complete, easy to understand manner ANY student of the Bibl,e who is teachable, will be able to pick up the entire Bible and see how this fits into God's complete plan for the ages. This is not just a doctrine. The Rapture is part of God's plan for the ages. My prayer is that the eyes of seekers will be opened. Once you understand God's order, plan and purpose, you will be happier than you have ever been, and you will face what is happening in the world with more of an eternal perspective than you ever have.

Mankind Divided Into Three Groups

God classifies mankind into three groups. Originally there were two and then with Jesus' resurrection, there became three:

The Jews. (Israel).
The Nations. (The Gentiles, nonbelievers)
The Church. (Born-again believers)

Understanding this will begin to straighten out many misunderstandings concerning the End-Time events and the Rapture. This is the way God sees it and it is very evident in scripture.

The first books of the New Testament: Matthew, Mark, Luke, and John, recorded Jesus life and ministry. Everything that Jesus said in those books, was not for every person that would ever exist. Jesus said, "I am not sent except to the lost sheep of the house of Israel." (Matthew 15:24) That was a dispensation, and that was His mission. He came there first. At that point His message was not worldwide although what He taught can be applied to all generations. The Jewish people were Abraham's natural offspring and God had made covenant with them. Jesus personally appeared to them and God fulfilled His promise to Abraham. We need to keep that in mind concerning End-Time events.

Let's consider Matthew 24: 1-51 and Luke 21:536, you will find Jesus laying the foundation from which most End-Time teaching has been derived. If you read it for yourself, you will find that his teaching on End-Time events was in response to specific questions He was asked. Another key is that He was answering them from the "Israel's" perspective.

Pardon me while I paraphrase. I do not want this book to just be copying and pasting scripture. Jesus had just walked out of the temple in Jerusalem and He said, "This temple will be leveled.

There won't be one brick standing on the other." Then when the disciples got alone with Him, they asked him three questions:

Final Call...Now Boarding

1. When will this happen? (The destruction of the temple which would happen in about forty years.)

2. What will be the signs of your coming? (Many see this as the time of the Rapture.)

3. When will the end of the world be? (The Tribulation and the second advent or return of Jesus after the Tribulation.)

All three of these events will not happen at the same time. In answering these three questions, Jesus painted a vast picture as to the future events concerning Jerusalem's future and the future events of the world and End-Times, and He gave us signs to help indicate the timing. Jesus' responses are recorded in Luke and Matthew.

I do want to emphasize this point. Jesus is talking to the Jews (Israel) about the Jews (Israel), concerning what they as a nation, race, and a people as a whole will experience. Some would be in the near future and some at the end. This should be read from a "Jewish" perspective. These are things they needed to know. Also, some of these can have a dual fulfillment. In other words, this means that the words Jesus spoke could apply to them not only for the present, but it could also apply for the future. I don't want to spend much time on this, but here is a summary:

- Jesus responded to the future destruction of Jerusalem in about forty years (See Matthew 24: 4-6;Luke 21:8-24)

- Signs of his "appearing" or rapture (Matthew 24:27:28, 32-51, Luke 21:29-36)

- The end of the world, Great Tribulation, and Jesus Final Return (Matthew 24:15-22,29-31; Luke 21:25-28)

My mission in this book is to not teach thoroughly on End-Time events, but to illustrate that when Jesus taught He was speaking of multiple future events. He also made reference to the Rapture event, however, because it would end-up applying to the Jews who had received Him as Lord when it takes place.

The New Testament Letters to the Churches

God's Word speaks to the Jews, the Nations, and the Church. Matthew, Mark, Luke, and John record Jesus' mission to save mankind, and his mission of being sent to the Jews. Following his resurrection, the New Testament Epistles or letters to the Churches were written and they are literally addressed, "To the Church… or Churches

at..." These would be from Romans to Revelation. If you read the epistles, you will find much revelation that was not in the four gospels. This also applies to End-Time events including the rapture of the Church.

Differences of Judgments

To once again illustrate the differences of the three categories of mankind, look at the judgments. There are three different judgments which the Bible teaches. By examining each side by side, you can clearly see they are not applying to the same thing. Let's take a look at them in order.

The Judging of the Church

After the Church has been raptured, she will be rewarded and with the rewards will come authority, position and placement in the Lord's leadership team for His government that He establishes here on the earth. Jesus gave hints as to this fact.

> "And behold, I am coming quickly, and My reward is with Me, to give to each according as his work is." (Revelation 22:12 MKJV)

> "Behold, I come quickly. Hold fast to that which you have, so that no one may take your crown." (Revelation 3:11 MKJV)

If you notice in these verses, Jesus referred to crowns and rewards. Crowns symbolize leadership and kingly authority. Jesus is referred to as "the King of kings, and Lord of lords." We will be the kings and lords and He will be King and Lord over all.

Paul describes the event of the judgment of the Church in 2 Corinthians 5:9-11 and 1 Corinthians 3:11-15. Remember that when he uses the phrases "all of us" or "everyman," that these epistles were written TO the Church. Additionally, you will not see the same events described in other judgments as a time in which rewards will be given for all our works we have done for Him. Our works will be tested by fire and those which remain will be rewarded. Even if rewards are lost, we will still be saved, because our salvation is not based on works.

The Judging of the Nations

At Jesus' final return at the end of the book of Revelation, all the survivors of the Great Tribulation who did not receive the mark of the beast will be brought before his throne. (Matthew 25:31-46) The Bible refers to that clearly as the "Nations" being judged.

The Great White Throne Judgment

After Jesus final 1000 year reign and Satan's final crushing, God the Father's Throne will come to earth. The sea, death and hell will deliver up all their dead and they will be judged by God the Father. Books will be opened and they will be judged according to all their works. Any of those whose names were not found written in the Book of Life will be thrown into the lake of fire to spend eternity.

Connection with the Rapture

These differences of judgments actually validate and again illustrate a connection to the rapture of the Church. Without studying the Bible, many just assume Jesus is going to come back and judge us, one and all at the same time. In each of these instances the people, location and times of these judgments are all different. With subtlety, the raptured of the Church is still implied. According to scripture, this is the explanation of how the Church is in a separate location being judged and rewarded, separate from the rest of the world.

In the previous chapter, we learned there were numerous raptures in the Bible, and realized there was a precedent for a great "catching away." In this chapter we established that the Bible classifies man into three groups: the Jews, the Nations, and the Church; and God's specifics of their plans and purposes are unique.

Now we need to look at the purposes of both the Jews and the Church. As we do, it will begin to solidify the foundational teaching that there is a pre-Tribulation rapture of the Church. There are multiple End-Time events and judgments. Everything must not be lumped in the same pile. Let's now move our focus to Israel and the Church.

Chapter 6

Israel And The Church

God's End-Time Vessels

LET'S GET TO THE HEART of the matter. God does nothing without an underlying purpose and plan. When we see God move, it initially strikes us as being spontaneous or unexpected, but every move the Lord makes has been meticulously calculated, and its ultimate outcome has been determined from the beginning. Our choices are not predestined, but God knows ahead of time what our choices will be. That speaks volumes of God's mercy, love and forbearance of mankind.

Final Call...Now Boarding

Israel's Plan and Purpose as a Nation

Does God's End-Time for Israel have any significance in the potential rapture of the Church? Yes, it does. Was Israel intended to be a mouthpiece for God? Yes she was. Was she instrumental at the Church's conception? Yes, she was. Will she be a mouthpiece for God once again? Oh yes, she will!!!! Glooorrryyy!! Let's answer some of these questions.

To look at what God had intended for Israel, we must go back to the time of her conception. The word "nations" was introduced in scripture in Genesis chapter 10, verses 20, 31,32. They were actually descendants of Noah's sons. In the next chapter occurred the tower of Babel, then the next chapter Abram (Abraham) was called. The tower of Babel was the only thing standing between the creation of nations and father Abraham.

When you look at God's call to Abraham and his covenant with him, it was a call that concerned nations. When God spoke to him initially, He told him, "I will make you a great nation." (Genesis 12:2 MKJV) A new nation was to be created. Later God changed Abram's name to "Abraham," which meant "father of nations." Why did God choose Abraham?

> "And the LORD said, 'Shall I hide from Abraham what I am doing, since Abraham shall surely become a great and mighty nation, and all the nations of the earth shall be blessed in him? For I

have known him, in order that he may command his children and his household after him, that they keep the way of the LORD, to do righteousness and justice that the LORD may bring to Abraham what He has spoken to him.'" (Genesis 18:17-19 NKJV underline added)

God knew Abraham's offspring would be a great and mighty nation and that all the nations of the earth would be blessed through that nation. Did you notice here the Lord also said that He knew Abraham would teach his children and future generations to keep God's ways. In essence, the nation that would come from Abraham would show the ways of the Lord and teach the pathway of blessings to the nations. They would be God's witness and light to the nations. That was God's original intention.

Jesus, the Fulfillment of Abraham's Promise

The Lord Jesus was the ultimate fulfillment of this promise to the world. In speaking to the Israel in John 8:56, Jesus said, "Your father Abraham rejoiced to see My day, and he saw it and was glad."(MKJV) Jesus was a Jew, a descendant of Abraham, a part of the nation of Israel, and His original mission was to the Jews. Jesus said, "I was not sent except to the lost sheep of the house of Israel."(Matthew 15:24 MKJV) Even when He sent out His disciples, He

Final Call…Now Boarding

said, "…Do not go into the way of the Gentiles, and do not enter a city of the Samaritans. But go rather to the lost sheep of the house of Israel.'" (Matthew 10: 5,6 NKJV)

For a moment let's even consider Israel's history in the Church so far. Jesus mentioned the word "Church" in the gospels only three times in Matthew 16:18; 18:17. In the first reference Jesus was stating that He was going to build a new organization, a new organism, a new body, it would be called "the Church."

The nation of Israel was the first to receive this message and was granted an invitation to become a part. The foundation of this new structure was the Twelve Apostles (who were all Jews), Jesus being the Chief Cornerstone. The entire word of God was penned and originally preached by Jews. God's heart was for this to have continued, but as a nation they rejected Jesus as the Messiah.

After Jesus was crucified, He was buried and was resurrected on the third day, He ascended to heaven, and offered his blood for the eternal redemption of mankind. Once completed, He returned to earth and established the Church with the outpouring of the Holy Spirit. He told his disciples that once the Holy Spirit had been poured out, they could now take his message to the entire world.

A "Church Age" is Clearly Seen

I believe this is so exciting and I pray that you will catch a glimpse of this. Jesus only mentioned the Church three times in two verses in all of Matthew, Mark, Luke, and John. Now here is what I find AMAZING. The word "Church" appears 111 times from Acts Chapter 1 thru Revelation Chapter 3, and that title IS NOT MENTIONED AGAIN throughout the whole Tribulation until Revelation 22:16. Now this speaks volumes, and I mean VOLUMES, to me!

When Jesus came to earth to preach the Gospel of the kingdom, his first message was recorded in Luke 4:17-21. This was the beginning of a new dispensation! He was quoting Isaiah 61:1, 2(MKJV),

> "The Spirit of the Lord Jehovah is on Me; because Jehovah has anointed Me to preach the Gospel to the poor; He has sent Me to bind up the brokenhearted, to proclaim liberty to the captives, and the opening of the prison to those who are bound; To preach the acceptable year of Jehovah"...(<u>He stopped quoting here</u>)..."and the day of vengeance of our God; to comfort all who mourn;"

He quoted this scripture verbatim and stopped in the middle of verse 2, and He closed the book, and He said, "This scripture is fulfilled in your hearing," but it was only fulfilled up to the middle of verse 2, He stopped and closed the book.

Final Call…Now Boarding

I believe that this refers to the beginning of the Church age. What did Jesus say would be preached? The "acceptable year of the Lord," but not the day of the vengeance of God. Why? Because it wasn't time yet. We are still in that time and dispensation.

What is the "acceptable" year of the Lord? <u>Thayer's Greek Definitions</u> defines "acceptable" as,

> "To take hold of, take up; to take with the hand; to receive; to receive or grant access to a visitor; not to refuse intercourse or friendship; to receive hospitality; to receive into one's family; to bring up or educate; *to receive favour*; give ear to; embrace; make one's own; approve; not to reject; *to receive, to take upon one's self,* to receive, *to get, to learn*" (Italics added)

The general context of the Greek word translated as "acceptable" implies - receiving, becoming, learning, being received into a family, and it is in a context of favour abounding.

I believe this describes God's graces and favor over the Church era, which we are still in. It's the time slot on the earth where God's graces are still freely open and accessible to us. In our age you can receive and become a child of God and be received into His family, as well as learn of the great salvation provided to us. It is the age where favour, not judgment is abounding. This is what Jesus described as the "acceptable year" which is the age of the Church.

In 2 Corinthians 5:17 thru 6:2, it speaks of born-again believers having received a ministry of reconciling men back to God, and a call to be ambassadors for Him in this earth. But He qualifies this as a dispensation. Look at 2 Corinthians 6:2, from the Amplified Bible.

> "For He says, In the time of favor (of an assured welcome) I have listened to and heeded your call, and I have helped you on the day of deliverance (the day of salvation). Behold, now is truly the time for a gracious welcome and acceptance [of you from God]; behold, now is the day of salvation!"

The age of the Church has been this time of salvation (deliverance, healing, preservation, soundness), and the time of God's aid, support and favour.

Israel's Purpose was clear

The Apostle Paul had a very clear understanding of Israel's place and her purpose concerning the fulfillment of preaching the Gospel. He preached that her destiny was separate from the Church's.

In the 11th chapter of Paul's letter to the Romans, he speaks to the election and destiny of Israel. He taught how they were cut off through unbelief (verse 20), and that through their fall they would be

Final Call...Now Boarding

provoked to jealousy that salvation had come to the Gentiles (verse 11). They are able to be grafted in again and they will be saved (verses 24,26).

A well known and frequently quoted scripture in Churches is, "The gifts and callings of God are irrevocable." (Romans 11:29) What is shocking about this verse is that in its proper context, it's referring to Israel! They are going to fulfill their call to preach the Gospel to the world and to be God's mouthpiece to the world. Do you realize how long the Lord has been waiting for this?

Paul does get a little more specific concerning the timeline of when this will occur. Let's look at Romans in the Amplified Version of the Bible:

> "Lest you be self-opinionated (wise in your own conceits), I do not want you to miss this <u>hidden truth and mystery</u>, brethren: a hardening (insensibility) has [temporarily] befallen a part of Israel [to last] <u>until the full number of the ingathering of the Gentiles has come in</u>."(Underlines added)

Paul referred to this as a "hidden truth" and a "mystery," and he said he did not want us to miss this. This is describing the end of the Church age and the beginning of Israel's. In Isaiah 60:1-3, God says,

> "Arise, shine, for your light has come, and the glory of the LORD rises upon you. See, darkness

covers the earth and thick darkness is over the peoples, but the LORD rises upon you and His glory appears over you. Nations will come to your light, and kings to the brightness of your dawn."(New International Version)

The Church is Unseen on Earth in the Tribulation

These verses are ultimately refer to Israel in her restored state, answering her call to be the Light to the Nations. As you study the book of Revelation, you will find that the Church is not even mentioned during the span described as the great Tribulation, referred to in Revelations 6 - 18. Could it be that she is not here? Wink, wink, nod, nod! Not including the two Witnesses, where is the fivefold ministry: Apostles, Prophets, Evangelists, Pastors and Teachers? The Church, which is growing in number as you read this, with some estimates being 2,039,000,000, and counting. Where are they? Hiding in caves and under rocks? I wouldn't be if I was here!!

Some may say, "They are the

martyrs underneath the throne." Almost two and a half billion would have to be martyred for the Church to not be mentioned. If we had as much faith in God as some have in the Antichrist, my what we would accomplish!

Where are missionaries? The Antichrist could not kill them all, especially taking into consideration, he will not have complete world control. His influence will be limited to 10 nations. A 200,000,000 man army will be coming to battle him from the east. These kings from the east, (probably China and Japan, maybe Russia) will help make up the final number present at the Battle of Armageddon.

The 144,000 and the Two Witnesses

At the beginning of the Tribulation, Russia will attack Israel with allies. God will defeat Russia (Ezekiel 38), the blinders will be removed from Israel's eyes, and God will call 144,000 Jews, 12,000 of all the tribes of the Israel to be His Servants (Revelation 7:1-3) and they are sealed and protected. Their converts will form a great multitude. Between 3 ½ and 4 years into the Tribulation, the 144,000 and their converts will appear in heaven. In Zechariah 8:23, the Bible prophesies a glimpse of this revival that takes place as the 144,000 Jewish Evangelists preach.

> "Thus says the LORD of hosts: 'In those days ten men from every language of the nations shall grasp the sleeve of a Jewish man, saying, "Let us go with you, for we have heard that God is with you."'"(NKJV)

At the 3 ½ years mark, God will send two witnesses and they will function as prophets. We do not know their identity. We already spoke about them in a previous chapter. They will be testifying the Gospel until they are killed four days before the Tribulation's end. They will not be killed, however, until their testimonies are complete, and until that time they will be immune to any of the Antichrist's attacks. The world will be witnessing all this via television.

So if you look at the whole Tribulation, God still has a plan for the Gospel to be preached, but as you can see, it's not the Church fitting that plan.

In review, this chapter shows how Israel has a specific place in God's plan. Even if you read from the Old Testament prophets (Isaiah thru Malachi) you find that in those books God speaks often of events that refer to the Jews for their future, even concerning the Seven-Year Tribulation. The book of Daniel is loaded. God was in advance declaring the end from the beginning, and preparing them for their destiny. When Israel comes to and shakes off her blinders, everything she will need to know are

Final Call...Now Boarding

written in the books that God already delivered to her.

In closing, I will again ask this question concerning the Book of Revelation and its teaching concerning the Tribulation: WHERE IS THE CHURCH? She's not mentioned!

Let's continue our journey and move on to our next lesson to answer this question.

Chapter 7

Jesus' Teaching On The End-Time Events

Answer Questions by Comparing Scriptures

MUCH OF THIS CHAPTER will be covering scriptures I was woken with on March 15th, 2009. In this chapter I will attempt to answer some of these questions: Did Jesus teach the Rapture? Is Jesus coming back to take His Church? If so, will He come before, during, or after the Tribulation? Are all the scriptures saying the same things? How can I know the truth?

Many of these scriptures can only be answered by comparing and studying scriptures. Every scripture that speaks of Jesus' return does not share the same fruit or characteristics, and sometimes do not even appear to describe the same events. The reason scriptures seem to contradict, is because they are not describing the same event. Let me give you an example.

In multiple scriptures the Lord's coming is described as a "thief in the night." (1 Thessalonians 5:2,4; Matthew 24:43; 2 Peter 3:10) When a thief comes in the night, he is stealth. He comes at time when the owner of the house is asleep or away, steals his belongings, and is gone before the owner realizes what has taken place. When Jesus comes as a thief in the night, it will bring the dawn of the new day, the great and terrible day, the day of the Lord, the day of the Great Tribulation, and the day of the vengeance of our God.

When scripture describes Jesus' second return at the end of the Tribulation, scriptures describe a different event. Revelation 1:7 states, "Behold, He comes with the clouds, and every eye will see Him," (MKJV Underline added). That does not sound like a thief! At this point He will touch down at the Mount of Olives, and will face His enemies at the Battle of Armageddon. This battle will mark the beginning of the end of the great and terrible day.

Did Jesus Teach the Rapture?

Before we look at what Jesus taught I want to be sensitive to those who may not be Christians, yet are reading this. When I was in Bible college, I was in a class in which the professor made this statement concerning the validity of Jesus. Jesus had many teachings on life, the hereafter, Heaven and Hell, salvation, healing, the Holy Spirit, forgiveness, faith, His Lordship, divinity, and the list goes on. How much faith we put in those words must be founded on who we believe He really was. Listen to what my professor said.

"With all Jesus said and did, He was one of three things. He was either a liar, He was a lunatic, or He was exactly who He said He was!" So I now ask you, the reader, these questions....

Was Jesus a liar?

Was Jesus lunatic?

Was Jesus who He said He was?

I challenge anyone living to prove those first two questions to be true. All of the major religions of the earth acknowledge Jesus as a great teacher or even a prophet, at the very least. If Jesus was who He said He was, and His words are true we need to take very, very seriously what He said and taught.

I believe Jesus, without a doubt, believed and taught the Pre-Tribulation Rapture. It is blended in with all His End-Time teaching, but we need to remember that the majority of His teaching on End-Time events was answering specific questions He had been asked. For the sake of this book, let's look at these instances concerning the Rapture.

Final Call...Now Boarding

Jesus' Teaching on the Rapture?

Let's start by reading Luke 17:24-37 (New International Version). These verses are so direct it's possible to receive revelation concerning the Rapture just by reading them without any additional commentary.

> "For the Son of Man in His day will be like the lightning, which flashes and lights up the sky from one end to the other. But first He must suffer many things and be rejected by this generation.
>
> "Just as it was in the days of Noah, so also will it be in the days of the Son of Man. People were eating, drinking, marrying and being given in marriage up to the day Noah entered the ark. Then the flood came and destroyed them all. "It was the same in the days of Lot. People were eating and drinking, buying and selling, planting and building. But the day Lot left Sodom, fire and sulfur rained down from Heaven and destroyed them all.
>
> "It will be just like this on the day the Son of Man is revealed. On that day no one who is on the roof of his house, with his goods inside, should go down to get them. Likewise, no one in the field should go back for anything. Remember Lot's wife! Whoever tries to keep his life will lose it, and whoever loses his life will preserve it. I tell you, on that night

> two people will be in one bed; one will be taken and the other left. Two women will be grinding grain together; one will be taken and the other left." "Where, Lord?" they asked.
>
> He replied, "Where there is a dead body, there the vultures will gather."

In verse 24 Jesus said it will happen at the speed of lightning from one part of the heaven to the other. In other words there is a flash of lightning, you blink and then it's gone, and He refers to this as "His day"!

"<u>As the lightning which lights up, flashing</u> from the one part under heaven, and shines." (Luke 21:34; underline added)

This describes the effect the Rapture will have. I believe literally the sky will be lit from its occurrence. Even more so, I believe the light, flashing and shining also implies the "revelation." Those who remain will receive after the Church's departure. Jesus describes this event as being the "day when the Son of Man is revealed," (Verse 30) not when he is "come," but when He is "revealed!"

<u>Thayer's Greek Definitions</u> defines this word "revealed" as:

1. to uncover, lay open what has been veiled or covered up

    a. disclose, make bare

2. to make known, make manifest, disclose what before was unknown

Final Call...Now Boarding

The Rapture is going to "reveal" to the world, both the Gentile and the Jew, that Jesus was who He said He was and what He said is going to happen was going to happen. The lukewarm church, those who were playing church, and those that heard preaching and never bought into the "salvation" idea, will have their eyes opened. The "revelation" of who the Lord Jesus Christ is will hit them face to face, and there will be much panic and fear.

Verse 25 says that before that happens He would be rejected by that generation, or the Jewish race, and thus the Gentiles' time would be in effect.

The verses following are where it really begins to get exciting. In verses 26-30, He gives us examples of the state our society will be in, and He shows <u>when</u> the "exit" would occur in relation to the pending Judgment! Look at how He starts the two examples.

In these two examples, He says, "As it was in the days of Noah, so it also shall be in the days of the Son of Man," (Luke:17:26) and "So also as it was in the days of Lot." (Luke 17:28).

Now remember these two instances are referring to the "appearing" or the rapture of the Church. Anytime I have ever heard these verses quoted the emphasis has always been that the sinful state of society be just as corrupt and destitute as it was in Noah's day and Lots' day. I believe there is more to grasp concerning when the Rapture occurs in relation to other events, and that these verses give real insight into God's heart concerning judgment. Both of Jesus' examples have many similarities, but first let's look at the instance of Lot. As we study this instance, it will become crystal clear what God's heart is concerning judging the righteous with the world.

Lot's Great Escape

As I studied in preparation for this book, thoroughly examined the story of Lot and Sodom and Gomorrah. This all begins in Genesis 18 in which the Lord and two angels pay Abraham a visit. The Lord re-affirms His promise with Abraham and Sarah both, concerning them having a child. Beginning at verse 16, as they were preparing to depart, the Lord stopped in verse 17 and said, "Shall I hide from Abraham what I'm doing?"(NKJV) What was it the Lord was doing? Let's look at verses 20 and 21.

"Then the LORD said, 'The outcry against Sodom and Gomorrah is so great and their sin so grievous that I will go down and see if what they have done is as bad as the outcry that has reached me. If not, I will know.'"(Genesis 18:20,21 NIV)

This had special significance to Abraham because his nephew Lot was dwelling there. God wanted to let Abraham know of the pending judgment, in essence, He gave him a "head's up." How does this relate to us?

We are Abraham's Seed

If we're part of the "Church", we are Abraham's seed, and heirs according to the promise. (Galatians 3:29) God can give us a "heads up" on coming judgment, especially one that will affect the whole earth. Jesus taught that the Holy Spirit would show us things to come. (John 16:13) Why did He show Abraham all of this? I believe so Abraham could play a part in saving whoever could be saved from the judgment! Does this sound similar to the Church?

Post/ Mid Tribulation Doctrine Inconsistent with God's Character

Now let's learn of God's character and heart concerning judging the righteous with the wicked. Look at these statements Abraham made describing God's character.

> "Then Abraham approached him and said: "Will you sweep away the righteous with the wicked?" (Genesis 18:23 NIV, underline added)

> "Far be it from You to do such a thing—to kill the righteous with the wicked, treating the righteous

and the wicked alike. Far be it from you! Will not the Judge of all the earth do right? (Genesis 18:23 NIV, underline added)

I want point something out here. Abraham knew the Lord as a righteous and good judge. People proclaiming that God's will is to test and pour judgment on the Church and World alike are grossly misinterpreting scripture and misrepresenting God. Abraham in his day had a better understanding of the heart and ways of the Lord. Twice, not once, Abraham said, "Far be it from You!"

During this whole scenario with the Lord, Abraham asks the Lord if He would destroy the whole city if there were 50 righteous…45 righteous…30 righteous…20 righteous…and finally 10 righteous. Each time the Lord said, "No." This clearly reaffirms his character and heart to Abraham.

God Never Changes

God has clearly told us in scripture, "I the Lord do not change, " (Malachi 3:6 NIV) and that He is the same, "Yesterday and today and forever." (Hebrews 13:8 NIV)

Once again I bring up the subject of setting a "precedent." Has God set one concerning the righteous and the wicked being judged together? Here we see one being set, and this is exactly why

Final Call...Now Boarding

Jesus referred to this example in referring to the rapture of the Church.

Stunning Similarities of Noah's and Lot's Story

The illustrations of Lot and Noah are descriptive of God's righteous means of judgment. The common thread between these descriptions was that the righteous escaped before judgment fell. Jesus uses Lot and Noah experiences as "types" as to the order of things pertaining to the Great Tribulation. In the days of Noah:

> "People were eating, drinking, marrying and being given in marriage up to the day..."(Luke 17:27 NIV)

And again with Lot He emphasized this point:

> "It was the same in the days of Lot. People were eating and drinking, buying and selling, planting and building. But the day Lot left Sodom...." (Luke 17:28,29 NIV)

Look at this and let this sink in. Life was depicted as going on as normal: people eating... people drinking...people marrying...people buying and selling...people planting and building. People were doing what people do. Life was going on. Then suddenly, in a moment, <u>in a single day</u> it all changed.

Look at what it says again with Noah:

"...up to the day Noah entered the ark. (Luke 17:27 NIV)

And with Lot:

"...But the day Lot left Sodom." (Luke 17:29 NIV)

Jesus then says, "It will be just like this on the day the Son of Man is revealed." (Luke 17:30 NIV)

What followed Lot and Noah and their family's being taken? Judgment. Look what Jesus said,

"...The flood came and destroyed them all." (Luke 17:27 NIV) "...It rained fire and brimstone from heaven and destroyed them all." (Luke 17:29 NIV)

God's Judgment of Sodom

It is also enlightening to go back and read Noah's and Lot's stories of God's deliverance. In Lot's instance, the Lord sent two angels to the land to spy out and confirm the extent of her state of sin and corruption. Their night's stay completely proved it was.

Look at what the angels told Lot in Genesis chapter 19.

"Do you have anyone else here—sons-in-law, sons or daughters, or anyone else in the city who belongs to you? Get them out of here, because we are going to destroy this place." (Verse 12, New International Version)

Final Call...Now Boarding

Lot was basically being called to preach at this moment, to say, "Judgment is coming, let's get out of here." When he went to his son-in-laws', they ridiculed him and thought he was joking. The next morning they received angelic escort out once they determined the town they were going to, and I want you to notice what the angel said.

> "Hurry! Run! I can't do anything <u>until</u> you are safely there." (Genesis 19:22 NIV underline added)

The angel said the impending judgment was being restrained not only until they were out but once they were safe in another place. Nothing could be done until they were gone. Scripture supports this same pattern of events for the Church in connection to the Great Tribulation. The Bible says that those judgments will be upon the whole earth. The <u>only</u> way to escape them would be to leave the planet.

Remember Lot's Wife

Throughout this story of Lot's escape, the angels said to invite others to accept deliverance. But there was also instruction given to them concerning their attitudes at the time of the departure. Jesus gave reference to in Luke 17:32, "Remember Lot's wife."

The angels had given specific instructions of how to depart in Genesis 19:17, "When they were outside, one of the angels said, "Flee for your lives! Don't look back." (NIV Underline added)

Lot's wife still had a love and a passion for the things of Sodom. She could not help herself. She looked back and began to wrestle with the decision to return. When she did the Bible said, "But Lot's wife looked back, and she became a pillar of salt." (Genesis 19:26 NIV)

Taken or Left?

Immediately after making reference to Lot's wife, Jesus follows this up with, "Don't try to hang on to your present life, because you'll lose it." (Luke 17:33) Then there will be two in bed…two grinding…and two in the field. One will be taken and one left. Does this sound like the Rapture?

Here Jesus is not only describing a vanishing rapture experience, but He is also revealing the heart attitude of those that would be left. He said, "Don't try to hang on to your present life." I'm certain there are many who wouldn't want Jesus to come, because they love their present lives, their things and their positions. All of these things are a deception and

Final Call...Now Boarding

cannot begin to compare with what the Lord has promised to and prepared for us who look for Him.

Lot's wife was convinced that her life in Sodom was better than where God was taking them. That is very hard to understand, because the whole city was filled with destructive perversion. What Lot's wife never realized was the reality that all she had known as her previous life was about to be destroyed. Once the Rapture occurs, life as we have known it on this earth will change immediately.

When the Rapture occurs life will never be the same on this earth again. It will be a time of judgment after judgment. Be willing to let go of this life and everything in it. Everything in this world is only temporary. There is no eternal value in it.

Finally Jesus ends this teaching with, "Wherever the body is, there the eagles will be gathered together."(Luke 17:37 Literal Translation of the Holy Bible) There have been many speculations as to the meaning of this verse. As I look at this scripture, I admit this verse could have multiple different meanings, but a specific experience comes to mind.

Beauties of the Mississippi

I live in Minnesota but until I lived here I never saw a real life Bald Eagle. Our city is surrounded by bluffs, and the mighty Mississippi River runs straight through it. A weekend out on the boat with my pastor gave me one of my first views of an eagle. It was soaring high over the Mississippi, and it was looking for prey. When an eagle prepares for a meal, it descends from extreme heights on an unsuspecting "body," silently and with extreme velocity. The eagle then "catches it's prey away" in one fell swoop. It will then ascend quickly back to its nest to feed its offspring. Then, and only then, does the banqueting feast begin. This is a picture of the rapture of the Church, and the "Marriage Supper of the Lamb" which will immediately occur.

There is a scripture back in the book of Jeremiah in which judgment is being proclaimed against the nation of Moab which utilizes an eagle as an analogy.

> The LORD says, "Look! An eagle is diving down from the sky. It is spreading its wings over Moab"... "The strong hiding places will be defeated. At that time Moab's soldiers will be filled with fear, like a woman giving birth."(Jeremiah 48:40,41 Easy to Read Version)

The Lord Jesus Christ is that great and mighty eagle. One day soon He will arise and descend from the nest like lightning and receive His own to himself. The shock of the Rapture will cause men's hearts to fail because of fear and unleash the Judgments of this fallen world system.

Final Call...Now Boarding

Parable of the Ten Virgins

Immediately following His teaching on End-Time events in Matthew 24, Jesus said, "At that time the kingdom of Heaven will be like ten virgins who took their lamps and went out to meet the bridegroom." (Matthew 25:1 NIV)

I encourage you to read this parable on your own in Matthew 25:1-13. Some Jewish historians parallel this parable to Jewish wedding customs. In other words Jesus was using an example they could understand. He said that at the time of the last days, it would be like these ten virgins. If ever there was a likeness the rapture of the Church, this is definitely it.

The primary characters of this parable are a bridegroom and his potential brides. I thought this was interesting by having a "Jewish Elope" planned and there being multiple brides. I can't imagine this going over too well with "the brides to be" on their honeymoon night. In Middle Eastern culture, multiplicity of wives may not be that far fetched, but taking them all at the same time would be rather odd.

In this entire scenario Jesus depicts a bridegroom coming to take his "brides to be" at a time they do not know and after a substantial delay (Matthew 25: 1, 5, 13). Some were "wise" (ready, expectant) and some were "foolish" (unready, unprepared)

(Matthew 25:3,4). The wise bought oil, the unwise did not. The unwise did not have the certainty, anticipation, and expectancy of the bridegroom's return, therefore they saw no need for oil. The wise lived with expectation and faith and they made certain their oil would not run out, no matter how long his coming was delayed. I see this as an issue of faith. Half believed He could come back at any moment, the other half did not.

Then suddenly a "cry" or "message" was proclaimed and heard, "Behold, the bridegroom is coming; go out to meet him!"(Matthew 25:6 NKJV)

All of the virgins heard this and they "woke up," "trimmed their lamps." This indicates a revival, a setting in order, and a beautifying of the Church taking place. The word in the Greek translated for "trimmed" here, is actually the same word we get our English word "cosmetics" from. This is again a perfect picture of a marriage. If a bride knew her groom was coming, she would get out her make-up, fix up her hair, and be wearing her most beautiful attire. This is exactly what will be happening in the End-Time revival. Only those who believe Jesus is coming with their whole hearts will read the writing on the wall. In a moment it will be all over and there will be no time to hash everything over, dissect all the doctrines, and even go to Bible college. You will not be able to live on someone else's faith. You must believe for your own self. We must get these things all figured out for ourselves right now.

I believe it is absolutely no coincidence that this book is in your hands at this moment. Please do not fall in to the category of the unwise virgins. Having our lamps full is being continually ready and expectant of the bridegroom's return. If your lamp goes empty, your light goes out. God's plan for you prior to the Rapture is for you to be a light source wherever you go. Shine and bring revelation to others.

The Door Will be Shut

Only the ones who were ready and watching and expecting him would be taken to be wed with Him. (Matthew 25:10) There is a point of "no return," a moment which we could refer to as being "too late." The brides missed their boat. The wise virgins make their entry to Heaven to the wedding and the door was shut.

What Time did it Occur?

What was this referring to prophetically? In relation to End-Time events when did it occur? From a timeline standpoint, it fits on at the beginning of the Tribulation. It could not have been at the end of the

Tribulation because it did not end with the Battle of Armageddon, but a wedding ceremony. (Marriage Supper of the Lamb) Could it have happened in the middle of the Tribulation? I don't' believe so because the bridegroom came at "midnight." Midnight, chronologically, is the last moment of time before the dawning of a new "day'. This does describe a certain event, and we need to strongly consider where it fits in with End-Time events. It will occur and it will be a trigger to the next dispensation upon the earth.

Another Striking Similarity

In Luke 12:35-40, we see another uncanny parallel. Keep in mind that the accurate way to Bible interpretation is to let everything be established in the mouth of two or three witnesses. Jesus is again making reference to the bride and the bridegroom, and the concept of marriage.

> "Be dressed ready for service and keep your lamps burning, like men waiting for their master to return from a wedding banquet, so that when he comes and knocks they can immediately open the door for him. It will be good for those servants whose master finds them watching when he comes. I tell you the truth, he will dress himself to serve, will have them recline at the table and will come and wait on them. It will be good for those servants whose master finds them ready, even if

he comes in the second or third watch of the night. But understand this: If the owner of the house had known at what hour the thief was coming, he would not have let his house be broken into. You also must be ready, because the Son of Man will come at an hour when you do not expect him."(Luke 12:35-40 NIV)

Jesus is describing an event when the Son of man will return, only for the purpose of taking people with Him and returning to a wedding banquet. He stated this will occur unexpectedly in the night before the day dawns. (Verse 38) He also said that if the owner of the house knew when it would happen, he would make an attempt to stop it. (Verse 39) In other words, Satan would do anything he could to undermine faith prior to it happening, because faith is the key to being taken. Remember Enoch, "<u>By faith</u> Enoch <u>was taken away</u> that he should not see death." (Hebrews 11:5 NKJV underline added)

We can escape the Tribulation

Jesus, without question, taught that we could escape the Seven-Year Tribulation. Look at how He ends His teaching on the End-Times in Luke 21:34 36. Let's read these verses:

> "Be careful, or your hearts will be weighed down with dissipation, drunkenness and the anxieties of

> life, and that day will close on you unexpectedly like a trap. For it will come upon all those who live on the face of the whole earth. Be always on the watch, and pray that **you may be able to escape *ALL*** that is about to happen, and that you may be able to stand before the Son of Man."(Bold and Italics added)

This was straight from Jesus' lips. He declared the Tribulation would come on the whole earth, and that it was possible to escape all that would take place and to be standing in His presence when it occurred. He also again used the word unexpectedly to describe the timing of this event, implying we need to live ready.

Now again let's look at Jesus describing the same event in Revelation 3:10-11:

> "Since you have kept my command to endure patiently, I will also keep you from the hour of trial that is going to come upon the whole world to test those who live on the earth. I am coming soon. Hold on to what you have, so that no one will take your crown." (NIV Underline added)

This was one of Jesus' final revelations to the Church at Philadelphia which I believe has a particular significance to the dispensation of the United States of America. These two verses contain a bulk head of information concerning the Rapture, End-Time events and even rewards.

Final Call...Now Boarding

Jesus describes that this church will be "kept." <u>Strong's Greek Lexicon</u> defines the word "kept" as "being detained in custody." Before you can be "detained in custody," you must first "be taken into" custody (the Rapture). They would be detained from what? The "hour of trial" (Tribulation) that will come on the "whole world."

I am no Greek scholar and I may not be the sharpest pencil in the drawer, but this is easy to see. This is not rocket science. What is the only way you can escape the effects of something that is coming upon the whole, complete, and entire earth? Wink, wink, nod, nod. I only see one answer. <u>You would have to leave the earth</u>.

Jesus Taught of Rapture and Post Rapture Events

In conclusion, Jesus did teach the Pre-Tribulation Rapture. However that was not all He taught. He also spoke to Israel of Post-Rapture events. Again remember His ministry was first sent <u>to the lost sheep</u> of the house of <u>Israel</u>. His purpose was to prophetically reveal to them what the future held for them. Too many Mid-Trib/Post-Trib believers have created a message for everyone out of Matthew, Mark, Luke, and John, that Jesus was intending for the Jews.

Let's move on to the next teacher of the Rapture, the Apostle Paul.

Chapter 8

Apostle Paul's Teachings On The Rapture

Uniqueness of Paul's Ministry

P<small>AUL'S TEACHING CONCERNING THIS</small> subject is very unique, especially concerning us. Paul was given the ministry to the Gentiles and his message was completely for the dispensation of the Gentiles. In his letter to the Church at Ephesus he said,

> "…I, Paul, the prisoner of Christ Jesus for the sake of you Gentiles— Surely you have heard about the administration of God's grace that was given to me for you, that is, the mystery made known to me by revelation …" (Ephesians 3:1-3 NIV Underline added)

And again,

Final Call...Now Boarding

> "...This grace was given me: <u>to preach to the Gentiles</u> the unsearchable riches of Christ..." (Ephesians 3:8 NIV underline added) Even Jesus had said this referring to Paul,

"But the Lord said to Ananias, "Go! This man (Paul) is <u>my chosen instrument</u> to carry my name before <u>the Gentiles</u> and their kings and before the people of Israel..." (Acts 9:15 Underline and parentheses added)

Paul had also referred to himself as an apostle "born out of due time." (1 Corinthians 15:8) Paul referred to the message he was called to preach. He said,

> "Now I want you to know, brothers, that the gospel preached by me is not based on a human point of view. For I <u>did not receive it from a human source</u> and <u>I was not taught it</u>, but it came <u>by a revelation from Jesus Christ.</u>" (Galatians 1:11,12 Holmen Christian Standard Bible Underline added)

Paul had revelations of things that the original twelve did not receive. That's why many things that Paul taught were exclusive to his books. He did, however, go to Jerusalem and submit his revelations to the original apostles as a point of accountability. Every minister needs a covering and a point of accountability.

Additionally, Paul's writings were the majority of the New Testament epistles. You may wonder why.

The reason would be because the Church age would cover the rest of time as we knew it up until the final seven years we refer to as the Tribulation. Let's go on to see what Paul said about the Church in relation to the Rapture.

The Church at Thessalonica

In Paul's two letters to the Church at Thessalonica, he addressed End-Time events, and without question described the Rapture. Even more interesting, however, he brings to the surface God's heart and answers why the creative idea for the Rapture was conceived in God's heart.

The Thessalonian Church had stress, anxiety, and confusion concerning End-Time events. We see that they had interest in the End-Time events, and that Paul had previously taught on the subjects when he was with them.

> "Don't you remember that when I was with you I used to tell you these things?" (2 Thessalonians 2:5 NIV)

He wrote these letters to strengthen their faith, calm their fears and to settle in them "the hope of His appearing." At the beginning of his first letter we see his heart bleeding through on this subject. It was part of Paul's foundational teachings with them. After Paul had initially preached to them, he later heard from the Macedonian church about their beliefs.

> "For they themselves report what kind of reception you gave us. They tell how you turned to God from idols to serve the living and true God, and to wait for his Son from heaven, whom he raised from the dead—Jesus, who <u>rescues us from the coming wrath</u> . (1Thessalonians 1:9-10 NIV Underline added)

Let those words settle in your heart, "Jesus, who rescues us from the coming wrath." Their testimony according to what Paul had taught them was that they would be rescued from the coming wrath. The Thessalonians believed this so strongly that they communicated this to the Macedonians. Jesus said, "That out of the abundance of the heart the mouth speaks." This was definitely something that was very strong in their hearts.

In 1 Thessalonians 4:14-18, you find what I refer to as the monumental verses concerning the Rapture. To any church go-er who believes in the Rapture, this is most likely their foundational scriptures:

> "We believe that Jesus died and rose again and so we believe that God will bring with Jesus those who have fallen asleep in him. According to the Lord's own word, we tell you that we who are still alive, who are left till the coming of the Lord, will certainly not precede those who have fallen asleep. For the Lord himself will come down from

heaven, with a loud command, with the voice of the archangel and with the trumpet call of God, and the dead in Christ will rise first. After that, we who are still alive and are left will be caught up together with them in the clouds to meet the Lord in the air. And so we will be with the Lord forever. Therefore encourage each other with these words." (1 Thes. 4:14-18 NIV Underline added)

In a previous chapter we covered these verses. Now I would like you to notice something specific. Paul said this message was, "According to the Lord's own word." Until now, the longest chapter in this book was the last chapter, which was Jesus teaching on the Rapture. Paul completely recognized and associated this teaching with the Lord Jesus Christ. After He describes the Rapture he goes on to make some distinctions concerning the saved and the unsaved.

The Bible's Most Powerful Pre-Tribulation Rapture Verses

When I was very wet behind the ears, and I was studying concerning the Rapture for myself, I received much more revelation from Thessalonians chapter 5 than chapter 4. When I studied this chapter the first time for myself I was seeking to know the truth. Studying this chapter was like having cement poured into the foundation of my belief system and I would never be the same. I would say these might even be the most powerful verses teaching the Pre-tribulation rapture of the Church in the Bible.

From chapter 5:1-10 look at the pronouns he chooses, and keep in mind that he is writing to the "Church" of which he is a member. He is comparing what will happen to "they" and "them" to what will happen to "you" and "us." It is subtle but undeniable. As you read pay attention to the pronouns.

He starts by telling the Church they must know the times and seasons they are in.(Verse 1) Then He says that they "know perfectly" that the Tribulation "Day" will come as a thief in the night.(Verse2) Jesus and Peter both stated this.

He goes on to say that when "they" (the unsaved) say, "Peace and safety," "sudden destruction" (the suddenness of the Rapture causes this) comes upon "them"(the unsaved) "as labor pains on a pregnant woman."(1Thessalonians 5:3) That is the exact way Jesus described it in Matthew

>24:8. "All these <u>are the beginning</u> of birth pains." (Underline added)

Initial Signs are the "Braxton Hicks" of End-Time Events

As Jesus described the end-times, He described the initial symptoms which would not be the "Tribulation," but precede it, just like birth pains prior to labor. This is just like what the delivery room specialists refer to as the "Braxton Hicks" contractions in child bearing. Prior to birth, Braxton Hicks contractions may be painful and can at times cause an expectant mother to believe she is in labor.

I clearly remember these types of contractions with the birth of all three of my children. Weeks before their birth, my wife and I would walk nightly. Even when we arrived at the hospital prior to their birth, my wife could have sworn that the baby was on the way.

As of the year 2009, I have been in "churchianity" approximately 37 years. Over just under four decades, I have seen many freaked out Christians at different times, even recently, who wondered if the horseman of the book of Revelation had already begun their rides. They are confused and have never taken the time to study for themselves what God has said concerning the order of End-Time events. If you study, you will have little question. We will see that Paul had to get more specific about this in his second letter to the Thessalonians in an attempt to get rid of their fear and doubts.

Final Call…Now Boarding

The "Braxton Hicks" contractions will be felt <u>prior</u> to the rapture of the Church. The true delivery contractions will occur <u>during</u> the Tribulation to "deliver the wrath." They will be very intense, very grievous, and very real. The Apostle Paul actually describes these birth pangs in verse three. He says the End-Times will be a topic of discussion. People will be wondering if this is the end because of what's happening in the world. Those in the world will even be saying, "Peace and safety, everything going to be alright," and suddenly, "Wham!," something triggers sudden destruction. It is the Rapture.

It ends with saying "they" shall not escape. (Verse 3) It says "they" will not escape…think about that…the implication is that we will. I encourage you to read and re-read this. Meditate on what you read and the Holy Spirit will give you revelation concerning these verses as He did me!

Then Paul says that "you" (the saved) are not in darkness, this day (Tribulation period) will not take "you" (the saved) as a thief! (Verse 4)

Before I bring up this final clinching thought, let's again bring to mind the context of all the scriptures we are discussing here. From 1 Thessalonians 4:13 – 5:11, Paul is speaking of End-Time events, but more specifically, he describes the rapture of the Church, and the day taking us as a thief. With that in mind, look at how he ends this discourse.

For God did not appoint us to suffer wrath but to receive salvation through our Lord Jesus Christ.(1 Thessalonians 5:9 NIV)

The word "appoint" used in this verse is defined by <u>Thayer's Greek Definitions</u> and the <u>Strong's Concordance</u> as: to set, fix, establish, to set forth, to establish, ordain, purpose.

This implies that having the Church (those redeemed or saved) go through the Tribulation is not what God has purposed, ordained or set forth. Instead His plan is "salvation" through the Lord Jesus. <u>Strong's Concordance</u> defines the word "salvation" as: rescue, safety, and deliverance.

Paul continues speaking of the Rapture in verse 10:

"He died for us so that, whether we are awake or asleep, we may live together with him." (1 Thessalonians 5:10 NIV)

Sounds like Chapter 4:15-18 is being repeated. Those asleep (the dead) will be caught up together with those who are still alive and remain. His train of thought has remained unbroken. To this point he has kept focus on this subject, and in verse 11 you will find his purpose.

"Therefore comfort each other and edify one another, just as you also are doing."

His motivation was so they could comfort and edify each other concerning the subject of End-Time events. These verses are intended especially for the people who would be alive when these events will take place. The Lord did not want His people worrying, fretting and fearing End-Time events, or wondering if they would be present during the Tribulation. None of these words would be "comforting" or "edifying" to us if we were going to face the "great and terrible day."

The Apostle Paul's Mission

When you read these letters that the Apostle Paul wrote to the Thessalonian Church, you can understand that part of his purpose to the Gentiles was to clarify End-Time events from their perspective, and more specifically concerning the Rapture. The New Testament Epistles were like God's final words to all the generations of the Gentiles, including us. Look at what he said in this first letter in chapter 5:27.

> "I charge you before the Lord to have this letter read to all the brothers." (NIV Underline added)

Paul knew that these revelations he had concerning End-Time events were important for the Church to grasp. You continue to see that in his second letter to the Thessalonians.

In his second letter to the Thessalonians, the central theme was to confront misunderstandings which had risen out of false teaching. Teachers, at that time, were proclaiming to the Church that they were already in "day of the Lord" (The Seven Year Tribulation), and that it had already come. The purpose for his letter was to combat this flawed theology and set the record straight.

In their presence, Paul had expended much effort to teach and admonish them concerning the Rapture. But now in his absence, they were receiving contrary "teaching, prophecies," and letters in the mail. This was producing some unattractive fruit, being shaken in mind and being troubled. Look at these verses:

> "BUT RELATIVE to the coming of our Lord Jesus Christ (the Messiah) and our gathering together to [meet] Him, we beg you, brethren,
>
> Not to allow your minds to be quickly <u>unsettled</u> or <u>disturbed</u> or kept <u>excited or alarmed</u>, whether it be by some [pretended] revelation of [the] Spirit or by word or by letter [alleged to be] from us, to the effect <u>that the day of the Lord has [already] arrived</u> and is here." (2 Thessalonians 2:1-2 Amplified Version, Underline added)

Here he is not speaking of one, but two different events that will happen simultaneously. This is a mystery!!! Confusion concerning these two events happens if you believe they are one and the same, even the Apostle Peter mentions that. Paul mentions them in the same breath because they will happen in the same breath so to speak.

Final Call...Now Boarding

Disbelieving the Rapture Produces Tormenting Fruit

If you believe the Church is going through the Tribulation, what kind of fruit does it produce? Let's look at this. The King James Version of the Bible uses the words "shaken" and "troubled" to describe this fruit. Let's see how Thayer's Greek Definitions defines these two words.

> "Shaken"–to shake down, overthrow, to cast down from one's (secure and happy) state, to move, agitate the mind, to disturb one
> "Troubled"- to cry aloud, make a noise by outcry, in the NT, to trouble, frighten ; to be troubled in mind, to be frightened, alarmed (Underlines added by me)

That is not good fruit! It is a state of continual torment. There is no peace. Why? Peace comes only from the Kingdom of God through the Holy Spirit, and the Word of God, and God's Word. The Holy Spirit cannot anoint doctrines and beliefs that did not originate with Him.

Someone may say, "Brother Jon, I don't believe in the Rapture and I have peace...I believe the Lord will take care of me through that time...because He's ordained it as a time of 'testing' for the Church." To answer that, I'll let Paul help me.

Untrue Ideals Disturb You Until You Believe Them

An ideal or principle that is untrue only disturbs you until you believe it. At that point what you are experiencing is false peace or deception. When you believe an "un-truth," you will no longer have the hope you once had. Paul did not call it a "different point of view," he referred to it as deception. Look at the very next verse:

> "Don't let anyone deceive you in any way, for (that day will not come) until the rebellion occurs and the man of lawlessness is revealed, the man doomed to destruction." (2 Thessalonians 2: 3 NIV, Underline added)

I am not questioning anyone's sincerity or motives who do not believe in the Rapture, or even if they are "believers." I am just pointing out that the central theme in the book is to re-strengthen the Church's belief system especially concerning the Rapture. Paul did not want their beliefs, concerning End-Time events, to be polluted with doubt. Faith is the key.

A Falling Away "From Faith" Will Occur

In the verse I just quoted Paul said that the "Day"(The Tribulation) could not occur until "the rebellion" occurs and the Antichrist appears. The New King James Version says it this way:

> "For that Day <u>will not come</u> unless the <u>falling away comes first</u>." (Underline added)

In 1 Timothy 4:1, Paul describes this falling away,

> "Now the Spirit expressly says that in latter times some will <u>depart from the faith, giving heed to deceiving</u> spirits and doctrines of demons." (NKJV Underline added)

We must remain grounded and in faith in respect to the End-Time events and what the Bible teaches about the Rapture. It's important that this is not lost from younger generations and future generations if Jesus' return is prolonged. The more important question, however, is what if we are the last generation? What if we are the generation to see these prophetic promises fulfilled? We must be confident, expectant, awake, and living life to the fullest as we look for His coming.

Paul goes on to say that before that "day" can be fulfilled, the "man of sin," or "son of perdition"(Antichrist), must appear on the scene (2 Thessalonians 2:3,4).

The problem is that something or someone is "stopping or restraining" this from taking place.

> "Don't you remember that when I was with you I used to tell you these things? And now you know <u>what is holding him back</u>, so that he may be

revealed at the proper time. For the secret power of lawlessness is already at work; but the one <u>who now holds it back will continue</u> to do so till he is <u>taken out </u>of the way." (2 Thessalonians 2:6-7 NIV underline added)

Paul said he had taught them previously. In looking at his teachings, more specifically the first letter to the Tessalonians this fits perfectly with the Rapture. Not only could the "Day" of tribulation not occur, but the Antichrist can not make his futile attempt of world control until someone is "taken out" of the way.

The "He" Taken Out of the Way

I believe the "he" that will be "taken out of the way" is the Church, Body of Christ. If you refer to a man with using the pronoun "he" you are speaking of him as a complete person, all he is, spirit, soul and body. Jesus is the "head" and we (believers) are His body. (Ephesians 5:22) Hence the pronoun "he" is used.

This is completely consistent with all the other scriptures Paul and the Lord Jesus taught. The Rapture will trigger the "and then" of future events.

"<u>And then </u> the lawless one will be revealed..."(2 Thessalonians 2:8 Underline added)

Final Call...Now Boarding

Notice the "And then" at the beginning of that verse. The words "and then" and "until the day" have a common thread through Jesus' and Paul's teachings on End-Time events. Both of those phrases imply that there is a sequence of events that will occur, not just one big boom. God is a God of order and as Abraham describing God's character said,

> "<u>Far be it from you</u> to do such a thing — <u>to kill the righteous with the wicked</u>, treating the righteous and the wicked alike. Far be it from you!"(Genesis 18:25 Underline added)

Let's now look at Peter's references to End-Time events.

Chapter 9

PETER'S TEACHINGS ON THE RAPTURE

THE APOSTLE PETER WAS probably the first pastor in Jerusalem after the Church was birthed. He also had a special place within the earthly ministry of the Lord Jesus in the Gospels. The twelve were always around Jesus, but it was Peter, James, and John that experienced special times with the Lord Jesus. Those three were present with Jesus when He was transfigured and Moses and Elijah appeared beside Him to speak to Him concerning His ministry. When Jesus went to the garden of Gethsemane, they were the three chosen to go on further with Him to pray. Peter was the only disciple to defy gravity and walk on water.

Final Call...Now Boarding

In the book of Acts, Peter was the one who had a vision concerning the Jews and the Gentiles in which God showed him there was now no difference between the two. I believe Paul probably had a closer relationship with Peter than the other apostles. After Paul's conversion, he went to Jerusalem and stayed with Peter fifteen days to tell him of his call to the Gentiles. They definitely had a closer relationship and Peter knew Paul had received revelation from God.

In 2 Peter, chapter 3, Peter did some teaching on End-Time events. He particularly referenced the events of the Seven-Year Tribulation and its end. I believe the reason he did not teach the Rapture in detail was because his call was not primarily to the Gentiles as Paul's was. He even deferred to Paul's teaching. I understand this completely. We have many teachers in our local church and all have their areas and subjects of strengths. Some teachers have more revelation on faith than others, some on healing, some on finances, and the list could go on. If a certain subject is being taught, you want the person teaching it that has strongest revelation in it. In Peter's second letter, he made brief reference to the Rapture and then he endorsed what Paul taught as "divine revelation." Let's start by addressing key points Peter shared concerning the Lord's coming in 2 Peter, chapter 3. You will be free to examine these in your own study time. I will just be touching on the highlights as they relate to the Rapture.

Peter starts in verse 1 by saying that we need to be "stirred up" (This means "fully awake") concerning the End-Times. He says that the way this transpires is as we are "mindful" or "remember" what the Apostles have written concerning the Last days. If you aren't fully awake, then you are lethargic and beginning to "nod off," and you don't realize what is happening around you.

Peter then made specific reference to the "Last Days" in verse three. He said that when the last of the last days finally arrive, there will be scoffers undermining the belief in the Lord's appearing. Look at how the "Message" translation states it:

> "...In the last days, <u>mockers are going to have a heyday</u>. Reducing everything to the level of their puny feelings, they'll mock, "<u>So what's happened to the promise of his Coming</u>? Our ancestors are dead and buried, and everything's going on just as it has from the first day of creation. Nothing's changed."(2 Peter 3:3, 4 Underline added)

The message of the Lord's return will be mocked and ridiculed. Was Noah mocked and ridiculed because of his message of a way of escape from an impending judgment? When time goes on and on and on, the hope and vision of a promise being fulfilled can fizzle and begin to "die out."

Final Call...Now Boarding

Peter then reminds us that God is eternal, and His concept of time is not like ours. A day with Him is like a thousand years. Then he goes on to say why there was a delay in His return. I love how verse 9 reads in the "Message" version:

> "God isn't late with his promise as some measure lateness. He is restraining himself on account of you, holding back the End because he doesn't want anyone lost. He's giving everyone space and time to change ."(Underline added)

Would God just allow all those who would receive Him to go through and suffer the Tribulation? No, He wouldn't. He is restraining this impending judgment for us, and for our salvation, so we can exit, as it comes "as a thief in the night." Look at part of that ninth verse again:

> "...He is restraining himself on account of you..."

Doesn't this have an uncanny resemblance to 2 Thessalonians 2:7-8?

> "Only He who now restrains will do so until He is taken out of the way."

Comparing these two verses again displays that the judgment is being restrained because of His love and mercy. He doesn't want His believers going through it. Additionally, the "he" (the Church) must be taken out of the way.

Jon Dowler

One of Peter's Most Quoted Verses

Probably the most quoted verse in 2 Peter is the end of verse 9, New King James Version states it like this:

> The Lord is "...not willing that any should perish but that all should come to repentance."

This verse is used by pastors and teachers for many different purposes, and rightly so, but when Peter wrote it, the intent was concerning End-Time events. He was teaching concerning the Lord's return and the Tribulation beginning. God does not want anyone to go through the judgment that will overtake the whole earth. His desire is that all would come to repentance beforehand and be ready to meet Jesus at His glorious appearing.

Peter's Final Thoughts on the Rapture

I am really amazed by Peter's last thoughts here concerning End-Time events. His very next words were:

> "Therefore, beloved, since you are <u>waiting</u> for these, be diligent to be <u>found by him</u> without spot or blemish, and at peace." (2 Peter 3:14 English Standard Version Underline added)

There is a word and a phrase I emphasized here. The first is "waiting." That word does not mean to just wait for something to happen. Thayer's Greek Definitions defines that word as this:

Thayer Definition:

1. to expect (whether in thought, in hope, or in fear)
2. to look for, wait for

Peter is saying that since these End-Time events are going to take place, we need to be looking for and in expectation of His return. The "promise" of His return is the primary subject matter in these verses.

The second group of words I underlined was "found by him." When you are found, that means someone came to you looking for you. When someone is looking for you there is always a purpose. You do not search for someone for no reason.

This verse says Jesus wants to find His people in a particular state: without spot, without blemish, and at peace. There is another scripture in Ephesians that goes hand in hand with this verse to complete the picture of what will happen at Jesus' appearing.

> "...To present her to himself as a radiant church, without stain or wrinkle or any other blemish, but holy and blameless." (Ephesians 5:27 NIV)

Coupling these two verses together He is coming to "find" a people to "present to himself." Sounds like the Rapture, doesn't it?

Peter's Falls Back on Paul's Teachings

In verses 15 and 16 Peter now brings together his teachings with Paul's.

> "Bear in mind that our Lord's patience means salvation, just as our dear brother <u>Paul also wrote you with the wisdom that God gave him</u>. He writes the same way in all his letters, speaking in them of these matters. His letters contain some things that are hard to understand, which ignorant and unstable people distort, as they do the other Scriptures, to their own destruction." (2 Peter 3:15-16 NIV Underline added)

In conclusion, Peter said that the Lord's patience means salvation. In other words, every minute that the impending judgment is prolonged for the earth is for the purpose of saving and delivering more people from that coming judgement. They had not heard this from Peter's mouth alone but also from the mouth of Paul. He said Paul had spoken of these events in all of his letters to them.

Paul had very strong revelations concerning the Rapture, and Peter said that those revelations were God given.

Final Call...Now Boarding

Paul's Teachings Hard to Understand for Some

In the book of Ecclesiastes, Solomon said "There is nothing new under the sun." All the debates have gone on and on and on. Peter said that some found End-Time events are hard to understand but he didn't say they couldn't be understood! Peter went on to say that because this lack of understanding, scriptures were being distorted by people that were unlearned and unstable, and destruction was the result.

Peter then points out that even people living in his day had a struggle believing in the events being described: The Rapture, the Antichrist, the Tribulation, when does the Rapture occur and so forth. In our day the controversy in the Church surrounding these events has centered on these questions:

"Is there a Rapture?"
and if so,
"When will it take place?"
(Pre-Trib...Mid-Trib...Post-Trib)

Let us move on and address both of these questions.

CHAPTER 10

WHEN WILL THE RAPTURE OCCUR?
(PRE, MID, OR POST TRIB?)

IF I HAVE DONE MY JOB to this point in the book, you should already feel like this question has been answered. The reason being, the teachings of the Lord Jesus and the Apostle Paul both have this intertwined throughout their End-Time doctrinal teaching.

"So Easy a Caveman could do it"

We've all seen those TV commercials selling auto insurance saying, "So easy a caveman could do it." Considering what the Bible says about the Rapture, I have already experienced a response like this from a person very close to me. With no hidden agenda, and a heart as pure as gold, I experienced a reaction similar to this from my 13 year old son.

During my studies of the Rapture over the past few months, he and I were awake far past his bedtime one night looking at some of the scriptures I have shared with you already in this book. I read him verses from Jesus' teachings and a couple of Paul's. When I finished reading him the scriptures, with hardly any commentary, he exploded, "How can people not see this... this is what the Bible teaches. How can anyone NOT believe this?" His response confirmed all my efforts in writing this book, and I came to the conclusion that this message is so clear anyone should be able to understand if they simply read their Bible and believe what it says. What we believe concerning End-Time events does matter! It affects our faith, our hope, our lives, and our families.

I was "Pan-Trib" in Attitude but not Doctrine

Many Pastors and spiritual leaders have not discussed these doctrines to avoid controversies. They may have a personal belief on one side or the other, but will not commit to a message. They will not commit either because of uncertainty, or by simply believing it just doesn't matter. They subscribe to the "Pan-Trib" theology, believing the End-Time events will "pan out" in the end and our beliefs can't change it. "What's the point in making waves?" In essence, I fell into that boat.

Up until this year, I avoided talking about anything slightly resembling any connection to the Rapture, when it will happen, and the Tribulation. There is some truth to "what I believe won't change anything" mentality, but that message will not hold water when time begins to run out.

If there really is a "rapture of the Church," doesn't it make sense that the message "Jesus is coming back" should marginally pick up a little bit of speed as the time is approaching?

If what I'm teaching in this book is true to scripture, it is inevitable that the dispensation of grace will come to a close. Would it make a "little" sense for people to be told beforehand so they can make an informed decision and be ready for it? Isn't this what God did in the times of Noah, Lot, and even Jonah? The Lord sent messengers who told them of what was to come and they had instructions on how to escape it. There is a precedent.

Final Call...Now Boarding

Lack of Persuasion Will "Silence" a Message

We must be persuaded. If these events will occur, we must believe in, expect, and anticipate His appearing being both wide awake and ready. Look at the question Jesus asked:

> "...When the Son of Man comes, will he find faith on the earth?" (Luke 18:8 NIV, italics added)

When we do not believe with certainty in the Rapture, then the message that "Jesus is coming back" is put to silence.

This brings us to the question, "When will the Rapture occur?"

Scripture teaches that specifically no man knows the...

> "...Day or the hour" (Matthew 24:38,42,44; 25:13)
> "...time" (Mark 13:33) "...times or seasons" (Acts 1:7)

According to scripture, anyone who tries to give you a date as to His return is in HERESY. If they ascribe dates to his return or appearing, they and their followers will be sadly disappointed. Jesus said not even He or the angels know the day or the hour. (Mark 13:32) Do yourself a favor and don't even go there. Just live ready!

Now onto the question you've been waiting for, "Will the Rapture occur before, during or at the end of the Tribulation?"

Jon Dowler

"It is **impossible** for Jesus Next Return to Occur during the Tribulation"

Was that sub-heading a misprint? No, it wasn't. I will fearlessly say it again. According to scripture, it is **impossible** for the Jesus next return (the Rapture) to take place during the Tribulation. I know by making that bold of a statement, I'm treading on thin ice by some people's standards.

When I was woken on March 15, 2009 at 4:00 a.m., I heard those very words in my spirit saying that it was impossible. In my world impossible is a strong word. Webster's Online Dictionary defines "Impossible" as- "Something that cannot be done."

What I experienced that morning when I heard those words is hard to describe with my vocabulary. I was taken back several steps by the word impossible. Impossible is not a very diplomatic word. I do not sit around from day to day attempting to dream up the most controversial ideas that I can.

When I heard, "It's impossible for Jesus next return to happen during the Tribulation," many thoughts immediately went through mind. I know from past experience that if God speaks something clearly to my heart, that eventually I will be called on to speak it. We live in a day of "openmindedness," and not having a closed, narrow point of view. Voices on every side scream, "We need to consider other peoples thoughts and ideas. We need to be open to new ways of thinking."

In general I would agree. As a manager in the business world, I prefer a team approach. When facing a conflict, a challenge, or a new venture, I want to get input from a substantial number of credible people before making any major decisions or pronouncements. I acknowledge that others can see a side of the mountain that I cannot. Valuing and considering their input could help save me grief, effort and efficiency. That is my heart. Even the scriptures encourage this principle:

> "But in abundance of counselors there is victory."
> (Proverbs 11:14 New American Standard)

When the word "impossible" was spoken, I was hearing, "This is not up for discussion, My mind is already made up, and it will happen no other way." In an instant, I could sense the reactions of people who had an opposing viewpoint. I could hear, "How dare you make such a statement?" or "Who do you think you are?" Then, before I could ponder this anymore, a great download began.

In what seemed to be about 15 seconds, all the scriptures I share in this book concerning the Rapture downloaded. I could see them all. It was almost like downloading an update to a program on your computer. I saw all the scriptures but I needed to read them for myself. It took the next three hours to go through the information that came to me in seconds.

This Message was not for me, but Others

As I meditated on these verses, I realized that the Lord's emphasis as to the chronological time of the Rapture was not just "for me." That was where the vision for this book began to conceive. Concerning this doctrine, God was "preaching to the choir," so to speak. My whole life as a Christian, I studied and believed in the Pre-Tribulation rapture of the Church I was completely persuaded. But to the point of telling everyone that it's "impossible" for it to happen any other way? Whoa!!! Give me a break God! The longest paper I ever wrote was in high school and it was a five page research paper. It's not as though this message is not controversial enough by itself without attaching the word "impossible."

As I started this chapter I told you that if I have done my job to this point in the book, you should already believe this message. But the Lord gave me key revelation in the scriptures and this is a clinching thought to bring the scriptures together concerning the Rapture. This was a major reason for this book.

A few pages previously, we quoted a number of verses in this chapter in which Jesus said <u>no man</u>, angel, or even Himself would <u>know</u> the <u>day</u>…the <u>hour</u>…the <u>times</u>…or the <u>season.</u>

What event are these speaking of?

Concerning Bible prophecy, we <u>MUST</u> account for these verses. Taking these and comparing them with other verses will clarify the way you view the timeline of events of Bible prophecy. If you really stop and spend some time meditating on this you will get revelation from the Lord and from scripture that will change your life.

Mid and Post Tribulation Doctrines Don't Hold Water

For all those who believe Jesus next return will happen in the middle or at the end of the Tribulation, we MUST qualify that belief with scripture. Jesus said we wouldn't know the day, the hour, the time or the season. Are those two viewpoints in harmony with each other? Can they exist together?

The revelation I received from the Lord proclaimed it was "impossible" for Jesus next return to happen during the Tribulation.

Mid-Tribulation Doctrine

The doctrine of the Mid-Tribulation Rapture coming of Jesus for the Church is vague and un-implied by any scripture. It is based on a "great multitude" appearing in heaven suddenly out of the Tribulation.(Revelations 7:9,14) However, if you read the 8 verses prior to the "great multitude" being mentioned, you can see there is a connection to the 144,000 being called, commissioned, and sent forth. This further illustrates they were converts of the Jewish evangelists.

I would like to add another thought here. Calling the "Church" the "great multitude" would be like me referring to my "wife" as "some lady." Take my word. That would not go over very well. We always have been and always will be called the "Church, the body of Christ." During that seven year period we don't even see the word "Church," not <u>even one time</u>. The "Great Multitudes'" appearance in heaven is a rapture (Being transported supernaturally), but <u>the Church was neither</u> the mouth-piece preaching the gospel here nor the great multitude that received the gospel.

Post-Tribulation Doctrine

In general the Post-tribulation theory believes that Jesus' next return will be at the end of the Seven-Year Tribulation. Some of those believe that the catching away of believers will happen simultaneously as He returns to earth. More specifically they believe that the believers who are still alive, will be caught up in the air to meet Him and then right back to the ground to witness the Battle of Armageddon.

Scripture clearly depicts events that do not fit into this theological picture. Jesus will indeed return to the Mount of Olives at the end of the Tribulation to engage the Battle of Armageddon, and believers will be with Him, but they will not meet Him in the clouds just prior to it. The contradiction here is so obvious, even a "caveman" could see it.

Not Knowing the Day, Hour, Time, or Season

In a nutshell, we just discussed both the Mid and Post-Tribulation beliefs. Their impossibility and flaw is tied up in the issues of time. Jesus taught explicitly that we would not know "the day, the hour, the time or the season." How can the Rapture occur during the Tribulation and the integrity of those scriptures be maintained?

I don't believe they can be.

I have thought and meditated long and hard on this very question, over the last 24 years. The cement of the word of God has fully settled in my belief system. I make no claim to be a specialist on the Book of Revelations, or all the End-Time prophecies in the Old Testament. I would say the "rapture of the Church" is my area of expertise when it comes to End-Time events. I've said it before, I'm not the sharpest knife in the drawer, but I believe I can bring some light to the subject anyhow. When the message of "truth" is spoken, and revelation comes, it results in freedom. That is my great desire for you.

Debates can be ended with a Bible and a Calendar

I believe the debates or at least a lot of them could be ended with a Bible and a calendar. If we take the Book of Revelation and seven years worth of calendars, we can see references to time, duration, and cessation. In other words, many events are not only described, but their beginning, end, and duration are clearly stated. God went out of His way to communicate that the judgment will end. It will cease and it will only go so far. If there was no end,

Final Call...Now Boarding

the remainder of the human population would be completely destroyed. The book of Revelations is replete with chronological references to time(days, weeks months, years) These references are throughout the book as buoys or markers so people will be able to know what will happen, when things will take place, and how long those spans will endure. What isn't present is His revealing, which occurs prior to the Tribulation.

Buoys on the Water

Our Pastor lives on the Mississippi River. He introduced my wife and I to the mighty river. We were hooked almost immediately. The breeze, the velocity, the smells, the sunsets, the eagles, the water... There is absolutely nothing like it.

Our pastor is always teaching. When we went out with him on his boat, we noticed buoys of different colors that float at varying distances up and down the sides of the shore. Each side had its own color which denotes the Minnesota or Wisconsin state boundary lines. He taught us that these buoys would signify rocks, water depth, or some other obstruction that could not be seen from the surface. They are markers declaring the point at which one thing ends and another begins. They were placed there for us to see and for our direction. In the day they were placed there, it was with the intention that the people who would go there would know what was hidden beneath the waters and what direction they were headed.

God's references to the durations of certain events in the Tribulation act as buoys on the water. These events indicate the boundaries of how long things will last. The Book of Revelations is very much informational concerning times and durations of End-Time events. It primarily covers a seven year period from chapter 6 through 19. We know from scripture that the Tribulation is contained within a 7 year span. It gives many descriptions as to time, and it is written as a roadmap to the Tribulation. Anyone on earth during the Tribulation could open the book of Revelation at any given time, and if they had any knowledge of current events they would be able to figure what point they were at in the timeline.

The 144,000 and the Two Witnesses

I could give many time indicators listed in the Book of Revelations, but my purpose in this book is to bring light to the rapture of the Church. I only want to look at John's revelation in light of clarifying the timelines, keeping it as simple as possible. Jesus shed light on His next return saying no man would know the "day," "hour," "time," or the "season." The book of Revelation does give specifics as to days and times, and most importantly, the Church is not mentioned.

Prior to the "earth damaging" judgments being poured out, the 144,000 Jewish evangelists will be commissioned and sealed with divine protection from any of the effects of them. (Revelations 7:1-4) I would like to add that if the Church were there, she would have been the one with this protection, but she has already been taken. The fact that these events are prior to major destructions confirms that the 144,000 get commissioned early in the first half of the Tribulation and then appear in heaven at the 3 ½ year mark or shortly after. (Revelations 14:1)

Mark Off the Days on the Calendar

At the 3 ½ year mark the two prophetic witnesses appear and they will be on the scene forty-two months or 1,260 days, which is exactly 3 ½ years on the Jewish calendar. (Revelation 11:2,3) Only after their ministry has been completely fulfilled will they be killed and their corpses will be left in the streets for 3 ½ days, broadcasted throughout the earth via satellite. (Revelations 11:7-10) They will then be resurrected and caught up, or raptured, into the heavens. (Revelation 11:12) Immediately following will be the return of the Lord Jesus Christ with "ten thousands" of His saints (Jude v.14) to destroy His and Israel's enemies in the Battle of Armageddon.

I wrote all that to prove my primary revelation, that it is "impossible" for the rapture of the Church to occur during the Tribulation. Like many people trying to "predict" His coming on a specific day, teaching His return or the Rapture as an event happening during the Tribulation is a prediction. If Revelations were to state Jesus' return during the Tribulation then you actually can predict it, thus Jesus would contradict His teachings by leaving no element of surprise, no mystery to solve. Again Jesus taught that we would not know "the day, the hour, the time or the season."

Jesus said be "ready," "awake," and "looking." Yet He said not to let the day catch you "unawares," or as a "thief in the night." He said not to think or say He was going to "delay His coming," and that He was coming at an "hour that you do not know."

Clearly those phrases do not mesh with Mid or Post-Tribulation theology because the Lord has provided specific timelines within John's revelation. Even the appearance of the Antichrist is at the beginning of the Tribulation, when he signs a peace agreement with Israel and then breaks his agreement at the 3 ½ year point of the seven years. (Daniel 9:27, the "week" is 7 years)

All of the evidence is inescapable, but thank God the Tribulation is not!

Final Call…Now Boarding

The Rapture is inevitable and it will occur. Jesus is coming back. His next return will trigger the seven year sequence of events that will end the dispensation of this world as we know it.

"So now what?," you may be asking, "What do we do now until He comes?" This is an exciting question to answer and I'll cover it in the next chapter.

CHAPTER 11

THE LAST GREAT AWAKENING

An Awakening "to God"

IN THIS CHAPTER LET'S TAKE a look at God's purpose, His plans for the Church, and for earth during the last of the last days prior to the rapture of the Church. The fire that burns in my heart is a culmination of several different messages for the last of days: the rapture of the Church, an unprecedented outpouring of the Spirit of God, and an awakening to God that will result in the most massive harvest of souls the Church has ever seen.

A "Great Awakening" to God will occur over the entire planet.(Haggai 2:6-9; Isaiah 60: 1-5; Acts 2:17-21; James 5:7-8). The miraculous will take place, conversions to follow the Lord Jesus will happen at epidemic levels. Supernatural healings, financial miracles, dreams, visions, and encounters and visitations of both angels and the Holy Spirit will be manifested, causing all humanity to see the entire and complete salvation that was provided through Jesus Christ.

However, I do want to issue a disclaimer here. I believe that Jesus could come before "today" expires. Paul and the early church were looking for His return around 2000 years ago. Jesus' message was to live ready and watching. We have already been seeing the effects of this "awakening" for a number of years. It will continue to intensify until it shakes every society of the world. God the Father will be the final authority of when enough is enough, and this dispensation comes to a close. Any delays are indicators of His mercy and His patience.

Webster's 1913 edition of the Dictionary gave this meaning of the word "awakening:"

> A·wak·en·ing
>
> a. Rousing from sleep, in a natural or a figurative sense; rousing into activity; exciting; as, the awakening city; an awakening discourse; the awakening dawn. -- A·wak·en·ing·ly, adv.
>
> n. The act <u>of awaking, or ceasing to sleep</u>. Specifically: A <u>revival of religion</u>, or more general attention to religious matters than usual.(Bold print added)

Jon Dowler

The word "awakening" has a very unique origin. From the website "Answers.com," the word "awakening" was a termed used and coined by Jonathan Edwards in 1736. Look at the history behind this word.

"In the winter of 1734-35, the mild-mannered Reverend Jonathan Edwards, minister of the Church in Northampton, Massachusetts, was astounded. People actually were listening to his sermons and following his advice. We are all sinners, he had said; our works will not justify us; God alone is the source of salvation. These words ended the "carnal security" of his congregation. Their talk turned to nothing but religion, and they began living godly lives. Even "the vainest and loosest"! Even young people! And this behavior was spreading from Northampton to other towns up and down the Connecticut River Valley." "In a famous letter published in 1736, Edwards called this a "general awakening." He used the term awakening because it involves awakening the conscience to the individual's state of sin and need for God's grace. There was, for example, "a young woman that had been one of the greatest company-keepers in the whole town, in whom there appeared evident a glorious work of God's infinite power and sovereign grace; a new and truly broken, sanctified heart." Edwards observed, "God made it, I suppose, the greatest occasion of awakening to others, of anything that ever came to pass in the town." "As it turned out,

Final Call...Now Boarding

this awakening of Connecticut Valley communities was just a prelude to what would be called the Great Awakening, which began in 1740. Stimulated by itinerant preachers, the Great Awakening swept back and forth through the colonies from New England to the South for many years. These awakenings set a pattern for American religious experience that continues to the present day, but the word we now use is REVIVAL (1799)." (Quoted from Ask.com, Word history of "Awakening")

The Awakening That Birthed a Nation

When this Great Awakening occurred, it changed the face of what America would become as a nation. From the 1730's through the 1770's preachers such as Jonathan Edwards and George Whitfield were used by God to transform all that this nation would be. George Whitfield became the best known and most recognized person in the Thirteen Colonies. There was a transformation and an "awakening to God" that occurred in which whole cities were converted and God's presence and peace rested over entire regions. It was said that you could walk through towns and hear Christians singing and praying from their houses. In 1776 the

Declaration of Independence was signed in Philadelphia, and God, through this "awakening" brought this country together as He intended it to be, "One Nation under God."

In less than 200 years, God brought into being the most powerful nation which had ever been. This nation has been the single greatest international influence for the spreading and financing of the Gospel.

Nay-Sayers and Judgmentalists

There are those that say judgment is coming on America, even that it already has begun. I understand that from scripture when the sin of a nation reaches the "full mark" that judgment would be necessary, because God is bound by His word. Anything less would make Him a liar. I also realize what I'm about to say may make some people, even Christians, very angry. I grew up knowing "judgmental" Christians very well. One thing to note is that those who are the most judgmental of others usually have more to hide in their own lives than those they are judging. My own life experience has proved this out. Look at what Jesus said:

> "Do not judge, or you too will be judged. For in the same way you judge others, you will be judged, and with the measure you use, it will be

measured to you. Why do you look at the speck of sawdust in someone else's eye and pay no attention to the plank in your own eye? How can you say, 'Let me take the speck out of your eye,' when all the time there is a plank in your own eye? You hypocrite, first take the plank out of your own eye, and then you will see clearly to remove the speck from the other person's eye." (Matthew

7:1,5 Today's NIV)

Judgmental people will pass judgment on others for "specks" while they themselves have "logs" in their own lives. That is a principle and I have seen that proved out in my own life.

God birthed America by a mighty awakening to God and He is not finished with her. America and the Nations will be awakened to God again. His presence will blanket entire families, neighborhoods, cities, counties, regions, states, provinces, countries and continents!

God's Judgment Would be Unmistakable

When I hear people say God is judging America, something on the inside makes me cringe. People and ministers need to be very, very, very careful when taking the place as a spokesman for God in declaring judgment on His behalf. Almost all of what people refer to as "God's judgment" is nothing more than the law of sowing and reaping occurring. God had told Noah that as long as the earth remained, so would the law of sowing and reaping. (Genesis 8:22) Paul echoed this in his letter to the Galatians,

> "Do not be deceived and deluded and misled; God will not allow Himself to be sneered at (scorned, disdained, or mocked by mere pretensions or professions, <u>or by His precepts being set aside</u>.) [He inevitably deludes himself who attempts to delude God.] For whatever a man sows, that and that only is what he will reap. For he who <u>sows to his own flesh</u> (lower nature, sensuality) will <u>from the flesh</u> reap decay and ruin and destruction, but he who sows to the Spirit will from the Spirit reap eternal life." (Galatians 6:7-8 Amplified Version, Underline added)

Do you see what that verse said? It didn't say God judged them because they sowed corruption. It said that when they sowed "to the flesh," they would "from the flesh" reap corruption. God has already set laws in motion by His word which He has spoken.

Were Adam and Eve judged by God when they ate of the tree of the knowledge of good and evil? No, but they still died spiritually at that moment and began the process of dying physically until they were deceased years later. Did God judge them? No, on the contrary, He was the one searching for them in the Garden afterward. Simply stated, the word He spoke to them just came to pass. He said that the "day that they would eat of it they would surely die." What they sowed they did end up reaping.

Jesus' Message was Awakening

In Luke 21:34-36, Jesus spoke on the end times, and more specifically, the Rapture. In these verses He predicts what would be prevalent at the time of the Rapture, what we needed to avoid and what state of mind we should be in. AWAKE!

> "Be careful, or your hearts will be weighed down with dissipation, drunkenness and the anxieties of life, and that day will close on you unexpectedly like a trap. ³⁵For it will come upon all those who live on the face of the whole earth. ³⁶Be always on the <u>watch</u>, and pray that you may be able to escape all that is about to happen, and that you may be able to stand before the Son of Man."(NIV Bold, italics and underline added)

Jesus said that in the "Last Days" we would need to be careful and cautious about letting our hearts be weighed down or burdened with <u>dissipation</u>, <u>drunkenness</u> and the <u>anxieties of life</u>.

If we examine these words, we find that our planet is full of what those three words represent. Let's define them and I'm sure you will agree.

- <u>Dissipation</u>- A headache (as a seizure of pain) from drunkenness (Strong's Greek Dictionary)

- <u>Drunkeness</u>-An intoxicant, that is, (by implication) intoxication: - drunkenness. (Strong's Greek Dictionary)

- <u>Anxieties</u>-Comes from two Greek words meaning to "divide" the "mind." The word denotes distractions, anxieties, burdens and worries. It means to be anxious beforehand about daily life. (Spirit Filled Life Bible, Word Wealth)

Taking definitions into consideration, Jesus was saying that in the Last Days the state of the earth would be inviting us to worry, be stressed, and to have anxiety. He was saying that there would be countless things to divide and consume our thought lives, and that the way much of the earth would deal with it would be with intoxication and drinking. This would not produce any real escape, but rather would bring painful headaches and horrific hangovers.

This Last Day Awakening will result in God's presence canopying regions for sustained periods of time. Signs and wonders will accompany it and the reality will be undeniable to those who witness them. The "good news" of the message of the Lord Jesus and His redemption will bring irrefutable evidence and supernatural change to lives of people, and the reality will shake communities.

I worked in the business world for a number of years, and with blue-collar, white-collar workers, and business leaders. Endless numbers come to work with a hangover, and are saturated with the burdens, cares, and stresses. Hours are being cut, cost of living increases, wages are being reduced, and expenses are rising, sometimes with every paycheck.

I want you to know there is no shortage of any kind here on earth; but this world is operating under a system that Satan governs. That system is condemned and the collapse of it is inevitable. It is a system that is bankrupt and the future it promises is one of debt, slavery and ultimately death.

One job is no longer enough, you must get two. Then that's not enough, resulting in both spouses having to work. God's kingdom operates on a different plane all together and it knows NO LACK! We will see it manifested in the lives of believers and shine like never before and millions will come to follow Christ and will be ready for His glorious appearing.

Peter Preached About It

In the book of Acts, Peter preached one of his most powerful sermons. The church had just been birthed out of a mighty outpouring of the Holy Spirit. There were many signs and wonders that began at that point and never entirely ceased even through today. Those 120 believers were in the upper room waiting for the outpouring Jesus had promised. That outpouring occurred on the day of Pentecost and it was not a one-time event but the beginning of the dispensation of the Church. There were thousands from many nations gathered in Jerusalem to worship at the festivals of Pentecost. When the Holy Spirit fell, there were signs and wonders. Those same signs and wonders, and the Church, overflowed into the streets as witnesses of God's salvation power. As they went into the streets, they preached to all those nations, supernaturally in their own languages by the Spirit of God. We do not get a line by line detail of what happened, but the Christians were accused of being drunk with wine. Why?? They must have been experiencing symptoms that resembled those of being drunk! Then Peter stood up and preached, arguably, his most powerful sermon ever, and as he did a Great Awakening occurred. Peter proclaimed:

> "...Pay attention to my words. For these people <u>are not drunk</u>, as you suppose, since it's only nine in the morning. On the contrary, <u>this is what was spoken through the prophet Joel</u> : And it will be <u>in the last days</u>, says God, that <u>I will pour our My Spirit on all humanity</u> ; then your sons and daughters shall prophesy, your young men will

Final Call…Now Boarding

see visions and your old men will dream dreams. I will even pour out My Spirit on My male and female slaves in those days and they will prophesy. I will display wonders in the heaven above and signs on the earth below…<u>before the great and remarkable day of the Lord comes; then whoever calls on the name of the Lord shall be saved</u>." (Acts 2:14-21 Holman Christian Standard Bible, Underline added)

I don't know about you, but even in those verses I am hearing, "rapture!" Peter was quoting Joel and he was referring to the Church's birth, inception, and the dispensation of the "Last Days." He then goes on to describe "Revival" and "Awakening." He also qualifies it with time markers, "Before the great and remarkable day of the Lord comes!"

He also says that whoever calls on the name of the Lord will be "saved" from that great and remarkable day!

The Lord Jesus is coming back very soon. A great awakening is coming, and has already begun. This will continue until every last person who will receive the Lordship of Jesus comes in and then "Bam"(Pardon me Emeril), Jesus will return for us!

So now the next question I can hear is, "So what should I be doing until that day?" Let's answer that in the next chapter.

Chapter 12

So Now What

What did Jesus Say?

IN PRIOR GENERATIONS, the message of the Rapture sometimes has produced "granola" Christians (Fruits, flakes, and nuts). Crazy things have been done in the name of the Lord. People have quit their jobs. Some have racked up credit card debt thinking they weren't going to have to pay it back. Over and over again people have ascribed dates to His return only to be shamefully disappointed. Some have been so busy standing and looking up into the clouds that they were no earthly good to us or any one else. In Jesus teaching concerning His rapture, He told us what to do and the attitude our hearts should be in. In Luke 21:36,

Final Call...Now Boarding

Jesus strictly warned to "Be always on the watch, and pray..."

"Watch" and "Pray"

He used the verbs "watch" and "pray." Vine's Expository Dictionary of Biblical Words defines the word "watch" as "to be sleepless, to be watchful." This implies to us that we are to be awake. We can not let what is going on in the world around us or even what is going on in our personal lives lull us to sleep. The Message version of the Bible says it this way:

> "But be on your guard. Don't let the sharp edge of your expectation get dulled by parties and drinking and shopping. Otherwise that day is going to take you by complete surprise, spring on you suddenly like a trap, for it's going to come on everyone, everywhere, all at once. So, whatever you do, don't go to sleep at the switch. Pray constantly ..."(Luke 21:34-36 Underline added) Look at how the Apostle Paul said it, "But there's far more to life for us. We're citizens of high heaven! We're waiting the arrival of the Savior, the Master, Jesus Christ, who will transform our earthy bodies into glorious bodies like his own. He'll make us beautiful and whole with the same powerful skill by which he is putting everything as it should be, under and around him."

(Philippians 3:20-21, The Message Underline added)

The Message says, "We're waiting the arrival of the Saviour." The King James Version says, "which we "look for." One says "look for," one says "waiting the arrival," and both are correct. Strong's Greek Definitions defined it this way,

"To expect fully: - look (wait) for."

Think about this, almost two thousand years ago, the Apostle Paul said he was looking for, waiting for, and fully anticipating the Lord's appearing! Additionally, three verses prior he said, "Join with others in following my example, brothers, and take note of those who live according to the pattern we gave you." (Philippians 3:17 NIV, Underline added) Part of Paul's conversation and example was speaking of the return of the Lord Jesus. We need to follow that example.

We need to be Operating in the Kingdom

What does operating in the Kingdom mean? In Luke 19:11-27, Jesus told a parable which was depicting himself "leaving" the earth and then "returning" for those servants to settle accounts. I want to place my focus on what He told them to do while He was gone. Let's read verses 12 and 13 in the Message translation:

Final Call...Now Boarding

> "There was once a man descended from a royal house who needed to make a long trip back to headquarters to get authorization for his rule and <u>then return</u>. But first he called ten servants together, gave <u>them each a sum of money</u>, and instructed them, '<u>Operate with this until I return.</u>'" (Underlines added)

Operate with what? Looking at this, the parable states this King (royalty) would leave and come back again. It then said he paid them all a "sum." I believe this is the "total package" a believer receives upon accepting Jesus as Lord. Let's read this for ourselves in Ephesians 1:13-14:

> "In whom also you, hearing the Word of Truth, the gospel of our salvation, in whom also believing, you were sealed with the Holy Spirit of promise, who is the earnest of our inheritance..." (Modern King James Version, Underlines added)

This is very explicit. If you are a part of the "Church," then you have heard the word and believed it, you have received the Holy Spirit of Promise in the new birth! Now look at what Paul called it. He said that the Holy Spirit is our "earnest." <u>Thayer's Greek Definitions</u> defines this word as: "<u>M</u>oney which in purchases is given as a pledge or down-payment that the full amount will subsequently be paid."

Does that go hand-in-hand with the parable Jesus was teaching? I believe so. He left us the Holy Spirit and His gifts for us to work in conjunction with us in doing the "business" of the kingdom. Now let's return to the parable, as he gave his servants the money, he said these words,

> "...<u>Operate</u> with this <u>until I return</u>."(Luke 19:13, Underlines added)

The King James says "Occupy." This is a revealing word. The root of this word in the Greek means, "To practice, that is, perform <u>repeatedly or habitually </u>(not just a single act); by implication to execute, accomplish, etc." (Strong's Greek Dictionary, Underline added)

We, as believers need to be in the act of accomplishing His plan and be "continually" in the process of executing it! Again look, He said, "Operate <u>with this.</u>" With what? With the person of the Holy Spirit! Romans 8:14 states that, "For those who are led by the Spirit of God are the children of God." (NIV) Not just a one time thing, this needs to be done "repeatedly" and "habitually." Until when? Until He returns! We need to be "occupying" and working with the Holy Spirit until He comes, not standing around gazing in the clouds. We must be instead making disciples in all nations until that day.

Final Call...Now Boarding

Don't say, "He's Delaying His Coming"

We have already looked at Jesus' teaching on the Rapture in Matthew 24: 36-41. A couple of verses later, however, He gives an illustration in the parable of the two servants. One was described as faithful and wise, the other is evil and bad.

From the standpoint of this teaching, I believe these two servants are like two types of "Pastors" or spiritual leaders. These are both men that receive authority to be over and in charge of "fellowservants."(Verse 49) This is very important. Pastors are "fellowservants" with those they are over in the Lord. The word "fellowservants" means "one who serves the same master with another."(Thayer's Greek Definitions) Being conscious of this will affect the way a Pastors feeds and ministers to the congregation He is over.

Another hint that these servants might be Pastors is that they were over his "household." This word comes from a Greek word which means "a household of attendants specifically where there is healing, curing and wholeness."

Now look at the attributes of these two leaders. Both of these are considered in the context of "when his Lord comes."

The wise and faithful servant is said to, "...give them their <u>food at the proper time</u>..." (Matthew

24:45 Underline added) This servant's message will be relevant to their time. This servant is aware of what is going on "at the time" and he feeds the flock accordingly. This implies that he has received insight from the Lord as to what is going on, and at the same time delivers the message the household needs to hear.

The Bible tells us what the evil servant is in verse 48:

"My master is delaying his coming."(NKJV)

"My master will not come just now." (Worldwide English New Testament)

"My master is delayed." (English Standard Version) "My master won't be back for a while." (New Living Translation)

"My master is staying away a long time." (NIV)

Looking at these different versions is making a strong statement. The evil servant "believed" his master was not coming NOW. Faith without works is dead, and he definitely backed up what he believed with works. He proceeded to, "...Beat his fellow servants and to eat and drink with drunkards." (Verse 49 NIV)

The word "beat" is not only a physical beating, but can also be translated as, "To wound, disquiet one's conscience." (Thayer's Greek Definition) The evil servant is not expecting his master to come, and it affects his own personal life, not just with food and alcohol but self seeking indulgence. Not pursuing God and His purposes as a spiritual leader, will always eventually result in wounding people and offending their consciences. How many people are no longer in church because spiritual leaders have beat them over the head with scripture, or lived a life of self indulgence that resulted in ruin. Look at how another verse describes this:

> "My lord is a long time in coming; and is <u>cruel</u> to the other servants, <u>taking his pleasure</u> with those who are overcome with wine." (1965 Bible in Basic English, Underline added)

The servant's attitude is not concerned about the well-being of those whom he is over but his own self-gratification. Intoxication can be caused by anything that results in a person's spiritual senses being dulled, and at that point the person is not spiritually sober.

Mid-Trib/Post-Trib Doctrine Communicates "He's Delaying His Coming"

Do you believe in the Mid-Tribulation, or Post-Tribulation rapture of the Church? If you do and you teach it, BY DEFAULT, <u>you are communicating</u> to others that, "<u>He is not coming TODAY</u>." If today were the first day of the Tribulation, <u>which it's not</u>, it would be as little as three and a half years or as much as seven years depending on which of those you would teach.

Am I saying that if you believe this doctrine, you are beating your fellow servants and living like a drunkard? No, no, a million times no! But remember that the word beat can mean to "offend the conscience." By teaching that He's not coming for three and a half to seven years, we are setting people up to stumble and inducing them to think that they do not have to address any issues they have in their lives at the present! A conscience offended is a conscience on the road to intoxication. Jesus spoke strong words to those who offended the consciences of His little ones! How much more critical is it, if your teachings influence people to miss the Rapture?

The Bible called this servant an evil servant. What does "evil" mean? One of Thayer's Greek Definitions defines this as, "...A mode of thinking, feeling, acting that is base, wrong, wicked." It could be said that this servant had a mode of thinking that was wrong! He was not thinking, expecting and believing the right way! I know this is a proper interpretation because look at how the Lord Jesus ended the story:

> "The <u>master of that servant will come</u> on a day <u>when he does not expect him</u> and at an hour <u>he is not aware of</u>. He will cut him to pieces and assign

him a place with the hypocrites, where there will be weeping and gnashing of teeth." (Verse 50 and 51, Underlines added)

Jesus said explicitly that this servant will not be expecting His return, and will not be aware of the hour. It can happen at anytime! This is why Jesus commanded us,

"<u>Therefore keep watch, because you do not know</u> on what day your Lord will come." (Matthew 24:42 NIV Underline added)

"So you also must <u>be ready</u>, because the Son of Man will come at an hour when you do not expect him." (Matthew 24:44 NIV Underline added)

All of these verses are referring to the same thing and they are even in the same chapter! We need to take the words of Jesus to heart. The fate of the evil servant was to be left with hypocrites and unbelievers and to have weeping and gnashing of teeth. There will be weeping and gnashing of teeth during the Tribulation and the final judgment.

So what is the final summary of this chapter? What do we need to be doing when He comes?

- <u>Occupy</u> – Be doing and living out God's plan for your life.
- <u>Be looking and expecting</u> – Incorporate this attitude into your philosophy.

- <u>Pray</u> – Stay in communication with God. He will keep you on the path.
- <u>Believe it could happen today</u> – Don't say or insinuate He will delay His coming.
- <u>Be ready</u> – Live ready to meet Him in a moment's notice.

Let's look at the last point in the final chapter. This was the ultimate purpose for writing this book. Yes, this book was intended to reveal the truth concerning the Rapture, but what if you are reading and you have not received Jesus as your Lord and Savior?

Chapter 13

Get Your Boarding Pass

Final Call...All Boarding

As I write this final chapter, my mind goes back to where it all began in the Minneapolis airport hearing these words, "This is the last boarding call for passenger Jon Dowler on flight --- to New York." The attendant actually called me by name. I don't believe that is normal protocol. Maybe she saw me on my cell phone and just figured that was me, but she was concerned enough about me missing the flight that she called me by name.

Final Call...Now Boarding

Are you on the Passenger Manifest?

I am telling you there is a flight getting ready to take place <u>very soon</u>! I did not tell you I believe it's going to happen, I'm telling you <u>it's going to happen</u>! When that flight occurs, only those on the passenger manifest will be going. Are you on the passenger manifest? Let me put it this way. This is an intergalactic flight. Do you have a current passport?

Jesus is Calling you by Name

I believe that if you got a copy of this book and you read it to this point, it was written specifically for you. Jesus is coming back again very soon. He is calling you by name right now. Will He come today...tomorrow...a year from now...ten years from now? Only the Father knows that.

Jesus came as a man and suffered and died for you, not only to make the way for you to go to heaven, but also live a victorious life here on the earth. Listen to what Jesus said concerning Himself:

> "The thief comes only in order to steal and kill and destroy. I came that they may have and enjoy life, and have it in abundance (to the full, till it overflows)." (Underline added)

Jon Dowler

God's plan is to bring life, peace, healing, restoration and joy to you. How do you receive this? You start by making Jesus your Lord.

In Romans 10:9,10, Paul said,

> "If you confess with your mouth that Jesus is Lord and believe in your heart that God raised him from the dead, you will be saved. For it is by believing in your heart that you are made right with God, and it is by confessing with your mouth that you are saved." (New Living Translation, Underline added)

If you are ready to start a new life right now, pray this prayer with me:

> "Father God, I come to you right now in the name of Jesus, because I recognize I am in need of a Savior. I believe Jesus died, was buried, and rose again on the third day. I confess Jesus as my Lord right now. Come into my life right now, and according to your Word, I am saved! In Jesus' name. Amen."

If you prayed that then give God praise right now! You are saved and you are now a child of God. Get into a Bible believing church and be living ready, expecting Him.

Jesus is coming very soon. Thank-you for allowing me to speak into your life!

About the Author

Jon Dowler has been involved in ministry since 1986. After attending Bible college, he pioneered and pastored two churches. He is a strengthener and friend of Pastors. He has been described a "Fire-Starter" with a prophetic edge. He excites and inspires people to experience the life of faith, and to have an intimate relationship with the Holy Spirit.

Jon resides in Minnesota, and is available for ministering in churches and conferences nationally and internationally. Jon has been married to Anita since 1986 and is blessed with three wonderful children: Sarah, Rachel, and Destin. For more information contact: www.overflowingliving.com.

About the Publisher

Leeway Artisans, Inc. was established in 2003 with the primary mission of providing Christian writers and artists the opportunity to publish works of literature, photography, and artwork of varying types. Our goal is to spread the gospel of Jesus Christ through creative products of inspirational value.

www.ingramcontent.com/pod-product-compliance
Lightning Source LLC
Chambersburg PA
CBHW070549050426
42450CB00011B/2788